Contents

Acknowledgements

Extracts taken from *Now We Are Six*, *When We Were Very Young* and *House at Pooh Corner*, by A A Milne, published by Methuen Children's Books and which appear in chapter 1 are reproduced with the permission of the publishers.

ETHICS

NURSING PEOPLE WITH SPECIAL NEEDS

Part I

Edited by

Verena Tschudin BSc (Hons), RGN, RM, Dip Counselling

Illustrations by Richard Smith

Scutari Press · London

First published 1994

British Library Cataloguing in Publication Data
Nursing People with Special Needs. – Part
1. – (Ethics Series)
  I. Tschudin, Verena II. Series
  174

ISBN 1–871364–85–X

Phototypeset by Intype, London
Printed and bound in Great Britain by
Athenaeum Press Ltd, Newcastle upon Tyne.

Contributors

Gosia Brykczyńska BA, BSc, RGN, RSCN, DipPH, CertEd, OncCert, RNT

Lecturer, Institute of Advanced Nursing Education, Royal College of Nursing

Terry Chandler MEd, RMN, RGN, DipN(Lond), CertEd, RNT

Staff Development Training Manager, Tameside and Glossop Health Services

Ben Thomas MSc, BSc, RMN, DipN, RNT

Chief Nurse Adviser, The Bethlem Royal Hospital and The Maudsley Hospital Special Health Authority

Stephen Firn MSc, BSc, RMN

Lecturer/Practitioner, The Bethlem Royal Hospital and The Maudsley Hospital Special Health Authority

David Grant PhD, MSc, BSc, Chartered Psychologist

Head of School of Creative, Cultural and Social Studies, Thames Valley University

Anne Manyande PhD, MSc, Dip Social Psychology, BSc, RMN, RGN

Lecturer in Health Psychology, Thames Valley University

Preface

Ethics is not only at the heart of nursing, it *is* the heart of nursing. Ethics is about what is right and good. Nursing and caring are synonymous, and the way in which care is carried out is ethically decisive. How a patient is addressed, cared for and treated must be right not only by ordinary standards of care, but also by ethical principles.

These ethical principles have not always been addressed clearly, but now patients, nurses, doctors and all types of health care personnel are questioning their care in the light of ethics. Their starting points and approaches are different, but their 'results' are remarkably similar. The individual person matters and the care given and received has to be human and humanising.

The way in which the contributors to this volume, and others in the series, address their subject is also individual and unique. Their brief was simply that what they wrote should be applicable to practising nurses. Each chapter reflects the personal style and approach of the writer. This is what gives this series its distinctive character and strength, and provides the reader with the opportunity to see different approaches working. It is hoped that this will encourage readers to think that their own way of understanding ethics and behaving ethically is also acceptable and worthwhile. Theories and principles are important, and so are their interpretation and application. That is a job for everybody, not just the experts: experts can point the way – as in this series of books — but all nurses need to be challenged and encouraged.

Emphasis is laid in all the chapters on the individual nurse and patient or client. Ethics 'happens' between and among people, and, by the authors bringing their own experience to bear on their chapters, they show how ethics works in relationships.

Great achievements often start with a small idea quite different from the end result, and so it is with this series of books. The initial proposal is almost unrecognisable in the final product. Many people contributed to the growth of the idea, many more were involved in implementing it, and I hope that even more will benefit from it.

My particular thanks go to Geoff Hunt, Director of the National Centre for Nursing and Midwifery Ethics, for his advice and help with this series.

Verena Tschudin

CHAPTER 1

Care of Children

Gosia Brykczyńska

Children are not simply small versions of adults. Children are people in their own right and with very specific needs, especially in hospitals.

This chapter starts with a study of the nature of childhood and then goes on to examine children's rights. Since 1979, the International Year of the Child, legislation has improved the lot of children generally, but as the section on the law and the child shows, legal protection is not enough to give children – and their parents – the care they need to help them become adults with dignity and the ability to make decisions for themselves and others. Resources and their allocation, as so often in this series, are questioned in the final section of this insightful chapter.

Introduction

There was a time when the ideal child was neither seen nor heard, and it did not occur to the world of science and medicine to intervene particularly and extend its concern for adults to the needs of minors. It is therefore interesting to note that in spite of this, there are several instances in the New Testament where Christ in his healing ministry is concerned with the fate of children – interesting, because whereas modern *medicine* appears to have its roots in ancient Greek and Roman, if not even Egyptian, medical tradition, modern *nursing* sees the dawn of its profession embedded in Judaeo-Christian biblical traditions of concern and compassion, which consciously extend to the welfare of children. Early nurses were the monks and nuns of Christian medieval tradition, and Florence Nightingale herself, the founder of modern nursing, was a deeply religious woman, much influenced in her professional work by Catholic nursing nuns and the German deaconesses of Kaiserworth.

In this multi-ethnic, multi-religious environment, paediatric nurses see themselves as a group of professional health-care workers who extend their concern and compassion in a most particular way to the care of the child and his or her family. In the Royal College of Nursing's (RCN) *Paediatric Nursing – A Philosophy of Care* (1992), the Paediatric Nursing Society of the RCN states that the paediatric nurse should 'recognise each child as a unique, developing individual whose best interest [should] be paramount.' Among the principles and commitments that the RCN considers fundamental to a paediatric philosophy of care are focusing on the needs of the child as an individual and co-operation and partnership with the family.

The nurse should 'consider the physical, psychological, social, cultural and spiritual needs of children and their families, while respecting the rights of children, according to their age and understanding, to appropriate information and informed participation in decisions about their care' (RCN 1992). These are the guiding principles of positive work with children and their families; however, these principles are not always followed, and moral disintegration and distress can ensue.

Ethical issues in paediatrics stem from at least three sources. They can be due to (1) intra-professional problems, e.g. the level and nature of paediatric nurse training; (2) inter-professional issues, e.g. the case of preferential monetary treatment of another health-care discipline over child health; or (3) the very nature of the subject-group with which the nurses are working. Children, especially children in need of health-care, present unique ethical problems to the paediatric nurse.

However, the uniqueness of children does not mean that ethical problems concerning them are in any way more spectacular or problematic than those encountered in other areas of nursing. All nursing is a *moral* art and the moral issues that arise in the course of professional work are as likely as not to be due to the extrinsic factors imposed by the patient group.

Nurses working with children will encounter many moral dilemmas and experience times of acute moral distress, but most of these instances will be due to a number of recognisable moral issues, those to do with negligent practice, disregard for truth, lack of fidelity, supporting questionable maleficent practices, etc. The most common root of all moral dilemmas, however, as experienced by practising nurses, is most probably poor communication. Inadequate communication between all parties involved, lack of patience, listening skills, bargaining skills and respect for differing views and opinions, all contribute to a climate where ethical issues become explosive and moral distress is rife.

Children are the objects of our special care. As with any vulnerable and fragile group, our concerns and care are that much more acute because we are not only aware of the benefit each child deserves, but also the necessary additional protection the child requires. The RCN document for paediatric nurses on the philosophy of care for children's nursing clearly states that the nurse 'continually works to identify trends which may threaten the health and well being of children' (RCN 1992).

The Nature of Childhood

Nursing children *is* different from nursing adults because children are entirely different from adults. They are, as Gaylin (1987) notes, 'incomplete adults'. The smaller the child, the more immature the young person may be, the more intrinsically different will be the approach of the nurse. A discussion of ethical issues in paediatric nursing must therefore start with the premise that children are *not* miniature adults, and clarification of such terms as infancy, childhood and the nature of the person must follow.

The notion that children are not simply small versions of adults is a relatively recent one, although even in antiquity it was recognised that childhood was not a carefree version of adult existence, but something rather awful, to be avoided at all costs! Thus Aristotle commented that 'no one in his right mind would tolerate a return to that sort of existence' (Aristotle 1215b). Children differ from adults physically, socially and psychologically, and certainly some social psychologists, such as Williard Gaylin, argue persuasively that for a higher primate, humans would appear to be born exceedingly prematurely. He comments that 'the irony in our development is that part of the uniqueness that makes us transcendent rests in the miserable, extended, helpless state in which we are born and remain for so long – is extreme, and unparalleled in the animal kingdom' (Gaylin 1987, p. 3).

Gaylin sees in the dependent state of infancy and childhood an interesting force for positive social evolution. He notes 'that the first year is controlled and dominated by our condition – the utter helplessness of the infant and *his* growing awareness of this dependent state' (Gaylin 1987, p. 4). The child is, however, neither passive nor ignorant of his or her surroundings, and the entire focus of the child's first year is to secure a guaranteed source of warmth, food and love. Satisfaction of these needs encourages the child to venture forth and explore the external world, but failure to find relief from hunger, distress, cold or pain results in retreat and a heightened awareness of a hostile surrounding and even personal danger. It is the child's total dependency on the adult world that dictates his or her reactions to external and internal stimuli, as Gaylin (ibid.: p. 4) notes, 'this biological factor establishes the earliest situation of danger and creates the need to be loved which will accompany the child through the rest of its life.' Now Gaylin (ibid.: p.8), like many other psychologists, states that this period of extended, biologically-determined dependency is a crucial period in the development of the child into an adult

> who loves and is lovable, who has emotions and relationships and who is capable of altruism and hope. For while all these attributes are biologically rooted, they will be psychologically encouraged or destroyed in the lessons of dependency learned in our peculiar period of extended helplessness.

It is usually the parents who satisfy the infant's primary

needs, and this parent–child relationship typically goes unnoticed. Only when disease or disaster strikes at the core of the relationship do we recognise how vital and how fragile the bond is. As Gaylin (1987, p. 12) comments: 'For the full development of a person, with sensitivities and sensibilities, with capacities to communicate and relate, a broader sense of nature is necessary. It is necessary to care for a child'. Much of this caring – 'loving' – is given by the nurturing parents but is done at a high emotional cost. One mother related how the removal of her infant from home to a tertiary care hospital caused her acute distress:

> The sight of Julia's empty cot opened the floodgates for me and let out all the pain and hurt of the day. The baby I had never been apart from, who should be snuggled in my arms now for a night feed was miles away, seriously ill and nobody knew why. It was almost too much to bear. (Cooper and Harpin 1991, p. 66)

The mother–child bond is indeed extremely close and biologically necessary if the human race is to survive.

The bond can be established even with an unborn child, and mothers of premature, sick or dying neonates talk of the incredible closeness the newly-born child can have with them, despite the child's obvious lack of the many essential characteristics of personhood, such as known sex, personal name or even specific characteristics. One mother giving birth to a premature baby of 25 weeks recalls:

> The nightmare begins, doubts harden, it's the baby, he's dying, NOT MY BABY, DEAR GOD, NOT MY BABY . . . my body fights to protect the child in me. NOT MY BABY, DEAR GOD, NOT MY BABY . . .
> 'Hilary! Hilary! your baby has to be born. If you want it to live you'll have to help us.' Yes, my baby is still alive, I WANT HIM TO LIVE . . . A baby tinier than a doll dangles in the air above me, limp. The same voice, calm

but commanding. 'It's a girl, look at your baby, we must take her away now.' He can't be a girl, that's our son; we've only thought about boys' names. (Cooper and Harpin 1991, p. 11)

The mother adds, in words too graphic to warrant additional comment: 'I am empty, numb, useless. There is no joy in this birth, only shock and disbelief . . . the unthinkable has happened: our baby, due next March, is born.' There is no denying the incredible closeness of mother and child in that personal account.

The closeness of parent and child can take various, more or less recognisable forms. One mother, recording her ordeal at a specialist London hospital where her son was receiving treatment for a congenital heart defect, found that, much to her amazement, the more energy she expended on clearing a flower-bed underneath the children's wing, the more energy seemed to flow into her son. After one particular complication following major corrective surgery, she recalls having to give consent for additional catheterisation of the defective heart and I

dashed back to what I now considered to be my garden and nature's description of David's heart. There in the middle was a huge lump of concrete which I'd just left at first weeding because it was hidden from view by a large bush. Now, with Chris's [her husband's] help, I removed it and all other residual debris. Then we went to wait, and as I tried to calm down the tense little traumatised heart that I felt beating just above mine, I became convinced that David would never survive another heart operation; the heart was just too frightened. In fact, I felt increasingly that David's whole being was frightened . . . (Cooper and Harpin 1991, p. 58)

The child took the necessary turn for the better. The mother adds,

To this day I do not know whether it was the catheterization

or removing that lump of concrete that did the trick, but
he had turned the corner while we were out. His toe
temperature had finally gone up and stayed up, and he
was doing a little of his own breathing. It was like a miracle
(ibid. 1991).

This incredibly intense identification with the child and
empathy towards him, coupled with the displaced psychic
energies spent on clearing up the flower-bed, formed a
unique, triangular relationship for the mother and child
with nature. Once the child was better and ready to go
home, she took him carefully wrapped up to see the
flower-bed, with its neatly kept rose bushes, little tree and
highland heathers. 'I felt the link in my bones where it
has been forged. I said goodbye to the garden and wished
it well; it had given me a lot . . . ' (ibid.: p. 60). The
mother adds as the final sentence to her personal account,
that her son 'still calls hugs, "gardens"!'

The recurrent theme running through these descrip-
tions of infancy and early childhood is that the child is
not a solitary being. The child only makes sense, takes on
a recognisable social persona and can be socially noticed
because in his or her dependency he or she is part of a
unique and special family group. Definitions of childhood,
notions of the child and concepts of personhood only take
on a moral significance because we, like the child, relate
to the external world in a social context. The child is part
of a family unit and it is this indivisible basic human unit
that is the concern and heart of paediatric nursing. The
child is part of a family, and in the family unit he or she
learns to love and trust the world. As Gaylin observes,
this is

> precisely because of our prolonged dependency. We would
> not survive as a species or develop as a type, were there
> not a social structure to support us . . . no theory of the
> nature of man is complete that does not recognise the

obligate social structure in which he must develop. (Gaylin 1987, p. 14)

Much of the young child's development in the family unit is achieved through play, where the tasks of life and struggles for independence are re-enacted and staged. The child projects his or her fears and concerns onto imaginary animals, playmates and any other person who happens to be around. It is through this mechanism of projection and primary transference that we have an insight into the magical world of childhood. Christopher Robin, in *When we were very young*, declares to his parents:

> I'm a great big lion in my cage, and I often frighten Nanny with a roar. Then I hold her very tight, and tell her not to be so frightened – and she doesn't be so frightened any more. (Milne 1989a, p. 17)

Acting out one's fears and emotions is one of the ways that children learn to come to terms with their emotions, but sometimes play-acting can be rather confusing, as when Christopher Robin thinks he is 'a Ticket man who's selling tickets-please, I think I am a Doctor who is visiting a Sneeze. Perhaps I'm just a Nanny who is walking with a pram, I'm feeling rather funny and I don't know *what* I am . . . ' (Milne 1989b: p. 9). Huizinga (1949), in his classic work on the social and cultural role of play, *Homo Ludens*, demonstrates that the intrinsic freedom of the child (like that of an animal) lies in his or her ability to play naturally. He states that 'child and animal play because they enjoy playing and therein precisely lies their freedom.' Children like Christopher Robin know that they are playing, they know what is real and what it is to pretend. Huizinga relates the story of a friend, who had found his 4-year-old son sitting at the front of a row of chairs, playing 'trains'. As he hugged him the boy said: 'Don't kiss the engine, Daddy, or the carriages won't think it's real' (Huizinga 1949).

Another important aspect of play for the child is the

notion of playground. There are physical or imaginary spaces set aside for the child where he or she is 'permitted' to play. It is a magical world within a larger, often cruel, world, which Huizinga says creates order. 'Into an imperfect world and into the confusion of life it brings a temporary, a limited perfection. Play demands order absolute and supreme . . . '. Certainly, watching children at play confirms the belief that nothing they do is haphazard or incidental, and that the notion of 'a space' where they can play, whether an area by their bed, the middle of the kitchen floor or a school playground, is an area they feel is sacrosanct and 'safe'. In the 1930s Piaget conducted his seminal studies on the moral development of children, having observed his own six children at play. The significance for paediatric nurses of the naturalness and need for children to play is that the hospital environment is not a natural milieu for the child to adapt to, and therefore nurses need not only to provide an area where children can play, but also to create sacrosanct spaces. This encourages the child's healthy moral development.

The healthy, happy infant grows and develops within a family unit at home and as this development takes place, he or she starts to play and investigate, test and recreate the world around him or her. Nothing could be more detrimental to the child and his or her developing personality and nothing could shake the parent–child bond more fundamentally than an enforced separation of child from parent, and transference of the child into a bleak clinical environment. It is the recognition of this reality (though still not fully recognised in all areas of the United Kingdom, and certainly not in many parts of the world) that has led to the publication of a succession of reports and directives on the welfare of children in hospitals, (Robertson 1958; Central Health Services Council 1959; Committee on Child Health Services 1976; Thorne 1991; Department of Health 1991b).

Failure to take heed of the essentially moral message of these reports, starting with the revolutionary findings of Robertson in the 1950s through to the latest government report written in conjunction with 'Action for Children', *Just for the Day* (Thorne 1991), would signify, on the part of the paediatric community, a gross incidence of moral harm. Allowing parents to accompany children in hospital, giving children the physical and psychological space to play and encouraging children to develop naturally is not a child psychologist's fantasy; it is the moral obligation of all those concerned with the total health and well-being of children. Efforts are currently being made to introduce more day surgery units, not just to facilitate the increase of minor surgical cases, but also in recognition that hospitals, even the nicest paediatric hospitals, are simply not the best places for children. This is essentially a moral response to a moral problem.

This chapter now turns to examine how a child's autonomy is interpreted by the most recent pieces of national and international legislation, notably The United Nations' (1989) Convention on the Rights of the Child (known as the 'Children's Convention') and the Children Act 1989 (Department of Health 1991a). These two pieces of legislation are shaping the moral directives on paediatric nursing practice and have profound bearing on the ethical position of children's nurses.

The Paediatric Nursing Society's 'Philosophy of Care' document (RCN 1992) pays heed to the articles of the Children's Convention 1989 and the Children Act 1989. Emphasising family co-operation, it advocates that the nurse 'recognise that good health care is shared with families and they should be closely involved in their child's care at all times, unless, exceptionally, this is not in the best interests of the child'. In support of parents' requests and for the good of the child, and based on overwhelming evidence of the benefits of this from child psychologists, paediatric nurses are requested to 'promote the right of children to have a parent accompany them during hospital-isation and treatment' (RCN 1992).

The fight on behalf of the children for the right to have their parents accompany them into hospital and into treatment rooms, anaesthetic rooms and on the wards has been long and hard. In most areas of the United Kingdom this is already the case, but each generation of health-care workers and nursing students has to be told this fact anew, and research evidence needs to be continually revised, updated and compiled, lest the apparent inconveniences and occasional problems involved with parents' complete access to the sick child cloud the thinking of health-care managers or health-care workers. Certainly, in many parts of the world, parents still do not have unrestricted access to the sick, hospitalised child, and in these situations informed paediatric workers must feel confident to defend the child's right to unquestioned access to his or her parents. As the RCN (1992) document points out, the paediatric nurse 'advocates the reduction of hospital admissions and in-patient stay by promoting family participation in care, day services and paediatric community nursing services.'

Children's Rights

The history of the United Nations International Children's Emergency Fund (UNICEF) Children's Convention can be said to have started not in 1978 in New York City during the International Year of the Child, but in the 1930s in Poland with Janusz Korczak, who wrote about great heroes, as he could have written about himself: 'The lives of great men are like legends – difficult but beautiful, (cited in Lifton 1988, p. 3). This, coupled with the wry statement: 'Reformers come to a bad end. Only after their death do people see that they were right and erect

monuments in their memory' (Korczak 1988), could
adequately sum up the greatness of this unique man.

Korczak, the *nom de plume* of Dr Henry Goldszmit, was
a renowned paediatrician, child psychologist, writer and
radio personality. Above all he was a friend and protector
of children. Many social historians have *written* on the
history of childhood, but Korczak made an effort to *change*
the image of childhood permanently. Korczak lived in
Warsaw in the 1920s and 1930s, and after giving up a
thriving paediatric practice, established a children's home
run on revolutionary democratic lines. The orphans themselves held their own 'parliament', controlled 'petty crime',
rewarded success and popularity, admonished 'wayward'
adult-carers and, together with Korczak, worked to establish a 'new kingdom'. The 'kingdom' Korczak had in
mind was elaborated on in his classic children's tale *King
Matt the First* (Korczak 1988). For the purposes of history,
suffice it to say that the principles he laid down in his
works on child psychology and development, such as *How
to Love a Child, The Child's Right to Respect* or *Rules of Life*
(Lifton 1988, p. 3), written between 1919 and 1930 and
recently reissued in an English translation, still hold true
today and should be made compulsory reading for all
child-care workers.

Korczak was Jewish, and at the outbreak of World War
II was held in the Warsaw ghetto, where he chose to stay
with the children of the orphanage in order to give them
support and guidance. In the summer of 1942, Korczak
and 192 children were deported to the gas chambers of
Treblinka. He stayed with his children to the very end.
He said: 'You do not leave a sick child in the night, and
you do not leave children at a time like this' (Lifton 1988,
p. 4). As one ex-Korczakian, interviewed by Korczak's
biographer, Jean Lifton, said:

You know, everyone makes so much of Korczak's last

decision to go with the children to the train. But his
whole life was made up of *moral decisions*. The decision to
give up medicine and his writing career to take care of
poor orphans. The decision to go with the Jewish orphans
into the ghetto. As for that last decision to go with the
children to Treblinka, it was who he was. He wouldn't
understand why we are making so much of it today (ibid.:
p. 9).

When considering ethical issues relevant to paediatric
nursing, above all we are deliberating on the necessary
level of moral development to be acquired and practised
by nurses, who are the moral agents responsible for the
welfare of children on their wards. UNESCO declared
1978–9 the year of Korczak, to coincide with the International Year of the Child and the centenary of his birth.
It was the Polish delegation at the UNICEF conferences
of 1978–9 celebrating the International Year of the Child
who put forward the request to draft an updated Children's
Convention. Ten years later, the UN International
Children's Convention was launched at the United
Nations' Children's Summit in September 1990 in New
York City. The spirit of Korczak permeates the Children's
Convention, the most important piece of international
legislation concerning children ever to be drafted. The
significance of this document cannot be overestimated.
Reflecting on the life of Korczak is never a time-consuming luxury on the part of child health workers, if as a
result they too put the child firmly at the centre of their
concerns.

Children, however, have not always been the focus of
adults' concern, and indeed the long history of childhood
attests to much hardship and abuse. Liz Ullman, comment-
ing on children's rights in the UNICEF (UK) information
sheet, notes that 'most children are born not with rights
but with threats' (UNICEF 1989). If we look at the ways
youngsters are treated throughout the world, from Africa

to Asia, from Latin America to Europe, from the slums of
Toxteth to the leafy suburbs of Cheltenham, at different
times, for different reasons, in different ways, children are
still being systematically abused and misused. They have
no basic rights yet, as the Nobel Laureates noted in Paris,
in 1988,

> if mankind is to realise the full potential of this planet and
> to pursue the dream of a future free from hunger, disease
> and fear, then it is imperative that we, as adults, recognise
> the needs of children and acknowledge our responsibility
> to provide for their survival, for their protection and for
> their future development. (UNICEF 1989)

Article 12 of the Children's Convention states: '**The
child has a right to express an opinion and to have
that opinion taken into account, in any matter or
procedure affecting the child.**' Article 12 could have
come straight from the works of Korczak. In his works
How to Love a Child and *The Child's Right to Respect*, and
in his stories for children, Korczak wrote: 'Children are
not people of tomorrow; they are people of today' (Lifton
1988: p. 355). Thus we respect children not because of
what they can become, but because of what they are *now*,
prompting Korczak to observe: 'who asks the child for his
opinion and consent?' (ibid.: p. 356).

Asking a child for his or her opinion, holding that
opinion as something sacred, and acting on a child's
opinion are all moral approaches towards a child which
demonstrate no social distinctions, certainly no moral differences between our approach to the child and our
approach to the adult. Not all philosophers, lawyers or
childcare or health workers, however, see the child in this
light. There is, in fact, a large volume of literature looking
at the *nature* of a person and the *nature* of the child.
Depending on the discipline, e.g. philosophy, biology or
psychology, different statements on the nature of the child

will be postulated. Usually, the nature of 'the person' is of technical concern to philosophers, for, in order to be considered a moral agent capable of free moral choices and therefore at least of some autonomous actions, the human individual must also possess the characteristics of 'a person'. With personhood go not only rights but also moral obligations; therefore, it is very important to know whether or not a particular individual is a 'full person' or not.

William Bartholome (1992), in an interesting and challenging chapter on withholding life-sustaining treatment in the context of paediatrics, notes the philosophers' obsession with definitions such as 'autonomous, rational agents', while the medical ethicist Engelhardt defines 'the person' for purposes of attributing moral responsibilities, as rather extreme. He states: 'I have never met one of those (and I hope I never do!).' And adds: 'I would rather use the concept of person in a much older, more traditional way; namely, that of a member of the human community: "one of us", if you like, a shorthand way of talking about persons' (Bartholome 1992, p. 21). It is imperative, however, that we clearly determine the moral status of a child, for our behaviour towards him or her will be governed by our fundamental beliefs and attitudes regarding children generally. Bartholome (1992) quite rightly points out that the word 'infant' literally means 'voiceless one', yet we should see and regard children as the most morally opaque members of our community.

More than any other members of our community, we cannot know what children 'feel', 'sense' or 'see' as right or good for them. The problem with children is that they occupy a fluid, transient position on the personhood scale; they are ever-changing and developing, no two children necessarily being at the same point of development at the same age. Bartholome resolves this by stating unequivocally that he sees children just as I see myself, as developing, evolving, (hopefully) growing persons. They are at a slightly earlier phase in the process than I, but I am still learning and I learn a great deal from them! This moral standing as developing persons requires that no one be capable (legally or ethically) of treating them as products, property, projects or pets.

It is crucial to respect the child we are nursing. If we only respected a child for what he or she will or could become, i.e. a rational (adult) free agent, then the child could not be morally nursed. Should the child never attain adulthood or maturity, as in the case of a child with a terminal illness, or an educationally delayed child, the logic fails. The very fact that children *can* be the victims of adults' transgressions, here and now, and not only in the future, is evidence that the premise that they are of value for what they *will* become, is at least partially false (Bartholome 1992).

The problem of trying to gauge the correct degree of autonomy to afford the child without completely paralysing the moral agent is a point brought up Daniel Callahan (1984), in a fascinating article entitled 'Autonomy: A Moral Good, Not a Moral Obsession'. Callahan sees autonomy as the basis for moral enfranchisement, that is 'establishing my standing as an equal in the community and my liberty to pursue my own ends . . . and the right to be spared the paternalistic interventions of those who think they understand my welfare better than I do. The purpose of autonomy is to make me my own *moral* master' (Callahan 1984; emphasis added).

In the case of children, it would appear that we cannot accord them *more* autonomy than they are capable of morally being responsible for. Thus a neonate is entirely without any moral obligations and is solely the recipient of human rights by virtue of his or her common humanity which he or she shares with me and his or her parents; but the neonate neither requests nor needs to be *morally* autonomous. The parents or carers of a neonate make choices on behalf of the child, not because they particularly want to (in a possessive sense) but because nature, as Gaylin (1987) would argue, has placed them in that naturally protective position. Callahan (1984) asks: 'does a respect for autonomy mean that we are not allowed to imagine a good for others beyond that which they imagine for themselves?' It would be an interesting argument that suggested otherwise.

As a child grows, so he or she matures in the moral sense, and Benson's (1983) observation that 'a common symptom of a lack of autonomy is undue anxiety about a slightly unfamiliar task' holds true not only for the anxious student but also the exploring toddler, for to be autonomous is, as Benson (1983) says, 'to trust one's own powers and to have a disposition to use them, to be able to resist the fear of failure, ridicule or disapproval that threatens to drive one into reliance on the guidance of others'. Using this definition, many adults are questionably fully autonomous, many will never reach an autonomous state and yet some youngsters (and minors in law) may already have reached this state. True autonomy increasingly appears to be something not only earned and treasured but a 'grace bestowed', a social attribute given to individuals in recognition of *their* own self-respect. The excesses of 'autonomous living' feared by Callahan (1984) have little to do with Benson (1983) when he points out that

autonomy, like courage – to which it is closely allied – is an essential virtue that everyone needs. It is not the virtue of a reflective aristocracy. It is essential quite simply because without it one cannot *live* effectively the life of a member of society . . . To be able to take charge of one's own life is an important element of a person's self-respect (emphasis added).

It is because we respect children and attempt to foster

self-respect in them that we try to accord them levels of moral, social and cognitive development. A child who is capable of a reasonable amount of critical (non-concrete) thinking can begin to be consulted and have important as well as trivial matters discussed with them. As Benson (1983) notes, 'the person who thinks for himself, who in short *thinks*, may also make mistakes, but has also adopted the method by which he may detect and correct them.' This statement holds true for most post-concrete thinking children and adults (if they too have reached that level of cognitive development!).

If we treat children as if they may have an opinion on a subject, for example, their impending surgery, treatment options, colour of theatre gown etc. (NAWCH 1992), we are treating children as if they are our moral equals and not as Bartholome (1992) suggests 'products, property, projects or pets'.

Article 12 of the Children's Convention enshrines the right of children to voice their opinion and thereby obliges adults to ensure that children are heard. Callahan (1984) echoes the question of many when he asks, does promoting autonomy mean that 'we are not allowed to persuade others that their autonomous moral choices are wrong or defective, or less valuable than they might be?' In the case of developing children this may be true, and as adults we would be morally inept if we did not attempt to point out to the *reasoning* child why his or her choices may not be the best. Callahan responds by saying that 'The moral autonomy of others does not rule out non-coercive attempts to persuade them to think or act differently. What we cannot do is to impose our values, or the dictates of our conscience upon them against *their will*' (Callahan 1984; emphasis added).

In respect of the care of children, all too often children have not been consulted on how they think about an issue, even if they could have responded.

Nurses often perform procedures on children without so much as a 'May I?' or 'When would you like me to come back/take your temperature?' etc. Fostering a sense of self-reliance and self-respect (if the nurse does not respect the child, why should the child respect himself?) is as much part of the paediatric nurse's work as practising technical skills. It is also her moral obligation as an informed moral agent.

Adults often fear that children will make mistakes, but informed children (and it is our duty out of respect for the children to inform them, before we ask their opinion or choice) will make no more mistakes and of no greater magnitude than a similarly informed adult at the same level of cognitive development. Mistakes will however sometimes be made, which is why Korczak said: 'there are no more fools among children than among adults . . . we renounce the deceptive longing for perfect children' (Lifton 1988, p. 356). But as with diabetic children who are 'allowed' to be 'autonomous' and invariably end up in a diabetic crisis, the wise child errs just once. Thus Korczak adds, the child has the right to '*a* lie, *a* deception, *a* theft' (Lifton 1988, p. 356) for this is the natural process by which the child learns to control his or her environment and above all, him or herself. Callahan (1984) observed that 'the trouble with wanting one's dreams to come true is that they may come true.' Children in the process of learning about the responsibilities of autonomy need to learn to temper their desires. Benson (1983) notes that 'to be autonomous in morality involves a greater degree of self-sufficiency than to be intellectually autonomous.' Moral autonomy is largely dependent on the level of social and cognitive development of an individual and is not fixed at a particular chronological age,

> for to be autonomous in one's thinking calls for intellectual skills, including the ability to judge when someone else

knows better than oneself. But it also calls for the ability to control the emotions that prevent those skills from being properly exercised. (Benson 1983)

Children and the Law

Paediatric nurses are aware of the nature of each child. They are familiar with the Children's Convention and accord as much respect to children and their families as they morally can (RCN 1992). Practising paediatric nurses in the United Kingdom, however, are also obliged to be familiar with national legislation. The most recent piece of legislation governing work with children is the Children Act 1989 (Department of Health 1991a).

The Children Act has not come about in isolation, but is part of a legal reform package, addressing issues in marriage, the family generally, the changing legal status of women and, last but not least, a series of High Court judgements concerning the limits of autonomy a youngster can expect. As British law starts to be challenged by international law, e.g. the Children's Convention, or the European Court of Human Rights, so the collective social statement on the nature of a child's autonomy in the context of the United Kingdom will be made clearer. Practising paediatric nurses, however, need to be practising ethically now, whether or not their moral conduct is explicitly condoned or encouraged by the law or the courts.

The Children Act 1989 is in many ways more family-centred than child-centred, which in the majority of cases is the way things should be. Health-care workers and the family form a partnership with the child, with the united goal of achieving the best possible care for the young patient. The patient, however, in paediatric nursing, is correctly understood to be not only the croupy toddler, but also his or her exhausted mother by the bedside, older siblings left at home with the dog and Gran, and a frantic husband who wants to know *now* whether or not he should sue the housing office for the substandard damp flat which they are renting, and should he show up at work tomorrow. Family care emphasised by the Children Act is not just a slick catchphrase for child health issues any more than for concerns over fostering and adoption. This calls for an enormous sensitivity and maturity on the part of health-care workers if they are to respond morally to the legal demands put on them, and that needs to be developed consciously in student paediatric nurses. Working with children will increasingly call for competence and courage, if not the occasional rule-bending rarely encountered or required in the *relative* security of nursing adults.

It should be ensured that parents are not separated from children even, or especially, at the time of a child's death. Yet as one mother recalls, her son

> Richard had not been dead half an hour. Tony [her husband] had been told it was the hospital rules that we vacate the room within an hour. Those words still echo in my mind. Hospital rules! I had heard them so many times over the past months and in my hour of greatest need they were still quoting them at me .... The nurse, who had been attending my son since his admittance to the ward, suggested we went home, knowing from numerous conversations with us that it was over a hundred miles.
> (Cooper and Harpin 1991, p. 118)

The point to remember in this account is not that rules may necessarily need to be broken but that there was a fundamental breakdown of communication here. For a fascinating account of ethically condoned, and indeed required, accounts of responsible subversiveness and rule-breaking, the reader is referred to Hutchinson's brilliant

study of this all too often 'hidden phenomenon' practised in Benner's term, by 'expert nurses' (Benner 1984, Hutchinson 1990).

As a consequence of this particular hospital rule, and in the absence of any other advice or solution proffered by the nurse, the mother, with the aid of her husband and the chaplain, started to strip the room of her boy's possessions. Her dead son was still lying on the bed: 'we stripped the wall of all our son's precious pictures and literally hundreds of well-wishers' cards. It seemed almost immoral to do this in front of Richard . . .' (Cooper and Harpin 1991, p. 118). The nurse, no doubt feeling a bit uneasy (if not foolish) about the situation, suggested that the parents return in the morning to strip the room, begging the inevitable question of why vacate the room in such a hurry, if it will not be needed until the next day? As the mother points out, far more generously than most others would have done in her position: 'I could not believe my ears. She was a kindly girl with the best of intentions but really did not have the slightest idea of how we felt. I could never return to that room'.

To treat the entire family as one unit is the aim of the Children Act 1989 and the aim of paediatric nursing. Sometimes, however, the family unit seems to have cracks in it; sometimes the child comes from a broken home, or a one-parent family or even a four-parent family, as is the case when both divorced parents remarry. To nurse a child in this context poses many ethical problems, as does nursing a child against the wishes of certain relatives, e.g. grandparents or an aunt or an older or younger sibling. However, although the child is nursed in the context of a particular family, it will be the welfare of the individual child that will be considered *most* significant. In no other area is this more emotive than in the area of informed consent.

The doctrine of informed consent, as presented by bio-ethicists, states that an individual has the right to be informed about treatment proposals and has the right to consent to specific treatments.

The philosophical debates surrounding the area of informed consent in adults are complex enough; the issues raised by fragile, vulnerable groups of patients such as children, the emotionally disturbed, multiply handicapped and individuals with learning difficulties, are almost unfathomable. It is, however, possible to find points of agreement, guiding principles, and legal pointers which at least begin to shape the thinking of paediatric health-care workers.

In the context of children and their families a child can give *assent* to treatment from the age at which he or she understands what is being discussed. The assent of a young child should not be seen solely as a moral luxury. Health-care workers do not seek the assent of a child because it is required by law (for it is not), or because it is seen to be the done thing (children would see through this very fast, as it would not be followed up by practice). Health-care workers seek agreement for treatment from minors, because they are respected as autonomous beings, and not as Benson (1983) would say, 'the products, property, pro-jects or pets' of various *other* moral agents. It would be questionable ethical paediatric practice to allow an ado-lescent *not* to have treatment, because such were the wishes of the parents. It would most probably be *illegal* and not only immoral if the wishes of the adolescent were not sought, especially if they should subsequently be found to differ from those of the parents. Not to honour a child's opinion in such circumstances would run counter to any natural sense of morality, if not common sense.

Parents or legal guardians are asked to give legal informed consent to treatment for minors under 16, pro-viding they can demonstrate rational concern for the child and fulfil certain criteria of reasoned ethical decision-making. Most parents have no problems fulfilling these criteria, and in any event, most children and minors agree with their parents' decisions, not just because of uncon-scious socialisation into particular patterns of thinking, but more significantly, because most parents want to alleviate the pain, distress or discomfort of their child, which is exactly what the minors would wish for themselves. Some-times, however, there are discrepancies; parents may not be guided by unbiased opinion or judgement and would wish to impose *their* wishes on what they perceive as *their* child. In instances like this, the guiding principle must be not what would *I* wish for *my child* but what would be best for *the* child. Korczak expressed this principle succinctly when he said, 'Love *the* child, not just your own' (Lifton 1988, p. 356), and in legal terms one could talk of deciding on the best interests of *the* child.

Decisions concerning the care of a child are all too

often made under extremely unsatisfactory conditions. As one mother said, watching her child's distress:

> she was getting weaker as we watched her. Suddenly all the fighting of the last few days seemed so futile. I felt deeply guilty for her pain and her suffering. She had fought so hard, and I had done so little for her. It was unreasonable to ask more of her − *but I needed her so much*, it was so hard to let her go (Cooper and Harpin 1991, p. 21; emphasis added).

Parents are often paralysed by the decisions they find they have to make. They are in fact only too aware that they are asked to make often irrevocable decisions concerning the life or death of their child, and in consequence feel that they are inadequate for the enormity of the task. Priscilla Alderson (1990), in a ground-breaking study of parents' consent to surgery for their children, talks about the emotional problems that proxy consent entails and, more importantly, what the consequences are when parents disagree with the medical establishment. Alderson points to the rarely voiced opinion that, as family separation is one of many possible complications of serious chronic illnesses such as childhood leukaemia, medical harm may exceed any benefit and 'family breakdown may then be a sign, not of weakness, but of a response to inappropriate use of technology if parents leave an intolerable situation' (Alderson 1990, p. 223).

Alderson lists a number of points which proxy consent entails, notably (1) the notion that it is informed; (2) that the consent be voluntary and consists of assessing potential harms and benefits; and (3) that the consent itself be 'valid enough', that is, given by an adult sufficiently capable of doing so. In the process of giving proxy consent, the health-care system may occasionally have to 'draw the line'. But most important of all, the proxy consent for a child, as with all adults' consent to their own treatment, must also entail a minimal level of understanding, choosing and finally knowing that it is possible to *refuse* to give informed consent, and/or to withdraw consent to treatment and/or research as appropriate.

In Cooper and Harpin's moving book *This is Our Child*, one of the children, Gavin, a 15-year-old boy, was diagnosed with acute myeloid leukaemia when he was 13. His mother commented that she wondered if it would be fair 'to put Gavin through the misery of months of needles, drugs, surgery, nausea and risk of additional infections when the prognosis was so poor' (Cooper and Harpin 1991, p. 83). She recalled how her husband insisted that Gavin know his diagnosis and share in the treatment plans because 'at age 13, Gavin should have a say in his future and that, however small the possibility of success, Gavin should not have the chance taken away from him even by us' (ibid.: p. 83). As treatment progressed and he responded to therapy it was time to consider the options for continued treatment with everyone he could. He then declared that he could not cope with having all the treatments again. He requested an alternative treatment of one dose of melphalan and then wanted to get on with his life again. His wishes *were respected* (ibid.: p. 90). What is so refreshing about this account is that Gavin's opinions *were* taken into account, his initial assent was upheld and his final refusal of uncertain therapy was also respected. The adolescent was treated as an emerging adult and respected in his own right, by both his family and the hospital.

Finally, in law, a child *may* consent to treatment against his or her parents' wishes: (1) when the parents are no longer parenting, e.g. in the case of runaway children and adolescents, or (2) when adolescents feel that they absolutely can no longer communicate with their parents, for example when teenagers became sexually active (however prematurely). The decision of the High Court in *Gillick v West Norfolk* would seem to indicate, as Lord

Scarman said, 'that parental rights to control a child do not exist for the benefit of the parent. They exist for the benefit of the child and they are justified only in so far as they enable the parent to perform his duties towards the child' (*Gillick v West Norfolk* 1985). This leads to the second instance when a child or adolescent may give consent to treatment, and that is when the parents' consent is invalid because it is 'unreasonable'. In such an instance the child's assent, together with that of an appointed legal guardian or maybe even alone, would be respected. A reasonable child or adolescent demonstrating all the competences necessary to make a decision about therapy, research or experimental treatment will probably be listened to more readily than an unreasonable adult not demonstrating sufficient competence.

These issues however are constantly being challenged and reaffirmed in the law courts. An example of a youngster *eventually* being listened to against the wishes of his mother came to light when a 9-year-old Danish boy challenged his mother's decision to have him hospitalised in an adult psychiatric hospital. He was *not* emotionally disturbed, but he preferred to stay with his father rather than his mother (they were divorced). The youngster was *seen* to be unreasonable and in need of treatment. This case of injustice towards a healthy minor was upheld by the European Court of Human Rights (1986).

Increasingly, children will not only be demanding their rights but will be challenging the system to achieve them. It will be interesting to monitor the new Children Act 1989 and the International Court of Human Rights to see whether children's rights will indeed be systematically and increasingly upheld. The forthcoming test of this will most probably be the campaign run by EPOCH (End to Physical Punishment of Children) to make illegal the caning and other physical punishment of youngsters.

Resource Allocation

Paediatric nursing is not immune to the general moral concerns arising from the need to ration and selectively allocate limited resources. In paediatrics, as in other areas of health-care, many ethical issues arise from the moral distress and anguish which result from limited resources, maldistribution of resources, or insufficient commitment to paediatrics on the part of successive ministers of health to assure an adequate supply of necessary resources. Paediatric nurses feel trapped by the conflicting demands of their job, that is, to perform their nursing duties adequately within an inadequate system.

Marginal services, such as child health services, often seem to compete with other health-care departments. Even when funds are apparently sufficient, the fact remains that funds come from a *finite* regional budget and adequate funds for paediatrics mean (most usually) inadequate funds for some other department. Eric Matthews (1992), in an interesting analysis of the ethics of health-care rationing, points out that 'the notion of rationing medical care seems to be intrinsically repugnant to many people. . . . Rationing is rejected as essentially unethical.' Paediatric nurses working with children increasingly experience moral dilemmas and distress which arise from having to work in what many of them regard as essentially unethical conditions. Matthews questions whether it is possible that rationing goods (even medical care) is inevitable. How do we make our decisions concerning resource allocations rationally and morally acceptable?

There is much talk about the lack of trained paediatric nurses, and especially about trained paediatric specialist nurses. This lack of specialists is directly affecting the delivery of health-care, especially tertiary care, to paediatric patients. As one mother stated:

there was such a shortage of nurses that they often had to use agency nurses to fill the gaps. The lack of staff had serious effects on us. The children were all very ill and most of them were waiting for major surgery, which often had to be delayed because of staff shortages.' (Cooper and Harpin 1991, p. 49)

Although it seems obvious to the paediatric community that children should be looked after by a qualified member of the paediatric team, the notion that anyone can take care of a child is still quite prevalent among many general-ists. It is this type of thinking that ultimately dilutes the necessary level of expertise needed to take care of very sick children, and calls into question basic ethical premises of health-care delivery.

The Royal College of Nursing Report *Specialties in Nursing* unequivocally states that if 'standards of care are to be maintained and improved, the profession has to recognise that specialist nursing means value for money for patients' (RCN 1988: p. 4). Otherwise, as the dis-traught mother noted, 'it was infuriating for waiting parents who knew that surgeons and theatres were free, to realise that life-saving operations were being postponed due to lack of nurses and for no other reason' (Cooper and Harpin 1991, p. 49).

It would appear, therefore, at least at times, that the fundamental ethical problem in paediatrics which is pre-requisite to so many other ethical problems, is the basic lack of sufficiently qualified paediatric nurses in general paediatrics and even more so in the high technology specialist areas, such as intensive-care work, transplantation medicine and neonatal surgery – to name but a few. Again, it is a parent who speaks so eloquently:

The nurses were over-worked and over-wrought. . . . They were dealing with anxious parents and the parents of dead children. The parents were miserable and the staff was short,

so we were expected to spend even more time in the ward
caring for our babies. (Cooper and Harpin 1991, p. 50)

There is something seriously wrong with our health-care
system if anxious parents awaiting cardiac surgery for their
children feel as if they 'have to' contribute to the care of
their child in hospital for lack of qualified nurses. The
level of distress and tension is evident by the incident
recalled by a parent, where 'ten minutes before [a child]
was due to go to theatre a critical case was brought in,
and they cancelled this child's operation. The father was
so upset he could not stop crying' (ibid.).

For the paediatric nurse, the ethical issues arising from
the lack of adequate financial resources to fund paediatric
units result in at least three moral problems.

First, inadequate funding for paediatric nursing personnel and especially highly trained paediatric nursing
specialists results in a second-class child health service or,
as some parents witnessed, in a non-existent service. There
are several socio-economic if not overtly political reasons
why the child health service is seriously underfunded.
However, saving on child health services to fund other
health-care departments is both shortsighted and counterproductive. Children kept well in the community and
nursed by specially trained personnel on a specialist paediatric unit will give far greater health returns and contribute
in the long term to a healthier population than children
left to their own devices and grudgingly serviced by a few
specialist nurses, should the child be hospitalised.

Children's nurses have become a very scarce resource
and student paediatric nurses need to be carefully fos-
tered and encouraged to specialise in their chosen paediatric field. Encouragement, however, takes moral
commitment *and* finances, otherwise it is an empty concept. Without sufficient trained paediatric nurses, children
will continue to receive inadequate or even dangerous

care. This is morally untenable. Never again should a parent have to comment that he was

> much impressed by this tired-looking but obviously very caring man [the doctor] who proceeded to tell me that he would not be able to help Richard [his child] at his children's hospital because of a lack of specially trained nurses. Transplant patients need intensive nursing, and although the facilities were available staff were not (Cooper and Harpin 1991, p. 101).

There are several reasons why there are insufficient numbers of trained paediatric nurses. Some reasons may be beyond the immediate control of health-care managers, such as the decrease in eligible school-leavers entering the nursing profession. However, other reasons are not only in health-care managers' control, but the problem is exacerbated by negligence and ineptitude verging on professional maleficence. In 1983, the Hutt Report confirmed some of the worst fears of the paediatric nursing community, presenting a regional example of paediatric nursing manpower problems, which was being repeated around the United Kingdom. It confirmed the suspicion that there were enough trained paediatric nurses in the country but that the majority of trained mature paediatric nurses found difficulties in finding employment in their chosen field (Hutt 1983). Ten years later, the situation has changed very little, with the new grading structure acting as a gate-control system to the employment of sufficient, *adequately* qualified paediatric nurses.

The problem of qualified children's nurses working with children is not limited to in-patient situations. In the community, financial cuts across the board instituted to help balance local health budgets mean abolishing school nurses' posts, paediatric district nursing services, community paediatric posts, etc. These paediatric positions were often fought for and established in the light of professional, governmental and consumer pressures for more sensitive and *cost-effective* approaches to child-care services in the first instance (Burr 1987; Meadows 1987; Central Health Services Council 1959; Committee on Child Health Services 1976).

Certainly, there are fewer children (per head of population) needing care than almost any other group of patients. This is due to their relatively low numbers (although they comprise about a quarter of the population) and overall low morbity rates. However, the inability of children to speak for themselves and to defend their health-care rights when they do need them, should not be seen as a legitimate reason for cutting their services. When children need care they often need highly skilled inter-vention – even so-called 'bread-and-butter' paediatrics calls for a sensitivity and understanding that does *not* come without specialist education.

Paediatric nurses need to be adequately trained, yet the current trend of consolidation of schools of nursing into regional nursing colleges has often left paediatric nurse education ill-serviced. Changes to general first-level nurse education were brought in before a thorough consul-tation with the paediatric nursing community about the entire range of children's nursing had taken place. This resulted in a haphazard approach to Project 2000 require-ments for initial child branch training, and to non-defined or ill-defined community education both in second-level specialties such as school nursing, health visiting, paediatric practice nursing and paediatric district nursing, and in tertiary medical paediatric specialties, for example, inten-sive care, oncology and renal nursing. Last but not least, no one is addressing the need for *specialist* paediatric nurse-educator training. These long-term manpower resource problems directly affect the efficacy of the work under-taken, for an ill-prepared and substandard workforce cannot deliver safe, efficient, competent, and caring practice (Brykczyńska 1992). Fortunately, there are signs that paediatric nurses are fighting back. Educationalists are beginning to run specialist paediatric basic and post-basic graduate nursing courses and paediatric community services are beginning to prove their worth financially if not ethically. There is however little room for complacency. In order to maintain the pivotal nurse–patient relationship, nurses and child health consumer groups need constantly to keep the interests of children paramount in the public's and government's awareness.

The second area of concern, reflecting scarcity of resources, concerns equipment and buildings. Increasingly, medical and surgical equipment is supplied by parent and consumer health groups. Sometimes the financial help encompasses the subsidising or funding of entire buildings (e.g. the new Great Ormond Street Hospital) or wings of a building, thus challenging the notion that health-care is freely available and paid from the nation's tax contributions. One might ask, why be concerned with how a particular piece of equipment or nursing post or building is funded? At its most basic level, financial arrangements like these leave the concerned parties uneasy, because of a certain element of vested interest in the deal. Additionally, an electron scanner, say, may *not* be the most crucial piece of equipment a hospital needs, or building a regional unit for children with cystic fibrosis may lead to a certain element of medical discrimination, an accusation already levelled at some adult patient groups. Finally, funding nursing and medical posts by private means within a public NHS calls into question the entire logic and philosophy behind *co-ordinated child-care services* as advocated by successive ministers of health, and is a very financially precarious situation – even more so than NHS-funded positions. This cannot be a good thing for the patient population.

There is one area of concern that affects the scarcity of a particular paediatric resource, and that is, organs for transplantations. The highly emotive appeals to the public for a liver or heart and lung by distraught parents or relatives leave the bemused bystander wondering whether he has indeed heard correctly. What is undoubtedly needed is an updated control register of tissue-types, potential bone-marrow donors, organs available for transplantation, etc. but somehow it goes against the grain of justice for health-care professionals (especially) to condone loud, emotive appeals by distraught parents, when these parents' wishes can only be accommodated by some other parents' distress. The entire area concerning organ transplantation is fraught with ethical pitfalls and moral quandaries (Fries 1989; HM Government 1989; Bryczkyńska 1990) and is the object of much serious debate. Paediatric nurses would do well to maintain their moral objectives to serve the families they are working with, if they work towards making an Organ Bank or Tissue Registry a reality; and concern themselves with promoting a general understanding among the public of the need for such a registry, while trying to discourage distraught parents from making public appeals.

An interesting ethical question arises when a child's organ is freed for transplantation, and is then used for an adult patient. Usually, parents do not specify the patient population group that a particular organ can be used for, and in some instances this concern is irrelevant. For example, cornea transplantations can be from adults to children as easily as the other way round, but a child's heart and lungs should really only be used for another child (histocompatibility being assured). What of the ethical implications (if any) of using a youngster's heart as an interim measure for an adult patient? Or the use of a neonate's tissue for research into a predominantly adult disease? These are but some of the professional issues that stem from a scarcity of resources, and paediatric nurses must feel comfortable in discussing them, since they will inevitably be confronted with them sooner or later.

The RCN (1992) document advocates that the nurse should

> promote the provision of hospital accommodation and facilities appropriate to the needs of children and young people and separate from those provided for adults . . . she/ he also . . . campaigns for accessibility and equity of health-care provision for all children while working to promote the development of comprehensive, integrated child health services.

This is no mean moral feat, but one that paediatric nurses must subscribe to if they see themselves as *children's* nurses. The privilege of working with children entails the obligation of fighting for their rights. Certainly central to the debate must be the RCN's recognition that the paediatric nurse 'asserts the right of all children in all settings to be nursed by appropriately educated staff and believes that staffing levels and skill mix must reflect the special needs of ill children and their families' (RCN 1992).

Philosophers from Plato and Aristotle through to modern bio-ethicists such as Peter Singer and Kenneth Boyd have tried to present a formula that can be used by the professional moral agent in trying to argue a case for an equitable distribution of limited resources. The most notable moral philosopher to present a theory of justice is John Rawls, who in a modified form of Utilitarianism argues for a particular method of just resource allocation (Rawls 1971).

Rawls would like to see a form of positive discrimination. He argues that there are occasions when the most just way to allocate limited resources is to allocate them *unevenly*. The poor individual needs more state financial help than the rich or wealthy individual, and the sick child may require more expensive treatment than a sick adult with the same disease, based on the child's particular physiological needs. Counter-intuitively, small paediatric or infant-sized equipment, medicine doses, etc., can cost several times more than the equivalent adult-sized equipment – but this is no *moral* argument not to produce small sizes or specialised equipment. Certainly, an understanding of some of the contemporary writings of modern moral philosophies can only help the distressed nurse in presenting a reasoned argument.

Conclusion

Ethical issues in nursing abound because nursing is a moral art practised among other human individuals, most usually individuals in some form of physical, psychological or spiritual distress or discord. Ethical issues in paediatric nursing are even more poignant, because the human individual concerned and central to the nurses' obligations, is in a vulnerable position *vis-à-vis* the nurses' undoubted power and control.

The question to grasp and constantly to ponder, however, is how and towards what ethical end do nurses wield their power and control? If the nurses use their position to foster the welfare of the child and his or her family, they have understood the fundamentally moral nature of their practice. Paediatric nurses care about their patients and clients, and their caring in turn becomes the manifestation of their moral commitment towards their young patients. The commitment is not a limited form of caring, but a constant, boundless commitment to the welfare of children; to all children and those in their care in particular. Like in the friendship of Pooh Bear and Christopher Robin, paediatric nurses are asked to promise to 'the child' that they will always remember and will never forget.

'Pooh, *promise* you won't forget about me, ever. Not even when I'm a hundred.'

Pooh thought for a little.
'How old shall I be then?'
'Ninety-nine.'
Pooh nodded.
'I promise,' he said . . .
'Pooh,' said Christopher Robin earnestly, 'If I – if I'm not quite – ' he stopped and tried again – 'Pooh, *whatever* happens, you *will* understand, won't you?'
'Understand what?'
'Oh, nothing.' He laughed and jumped to his feet.
'Come on!'
'Where?' said Pooh.
'Anywhere,' said Christopher Robin.'
(Milne 1989c, p. 175)

And it is to 'anywhere' that the paediatric nurse must be prepared to go, with the sick, bewildered, lost or angry child.

References

Alderson P (1990) *Choosing for Children*. Oxford: Oxford University Press.
Aristotle, How should a man live? From: *Eudomian Ethics* 1215b, pp 202–13. In O Hanfling (ed.) (1988) *Life and Meaning: A Reader*. Oxford: Basil Blackwell.
Bartholome W (1992) Withholding/withdrawing life-sustaining treatment. In M M Burgess and B E Woodrow (eds) *Contemporary Issues in Paediatric Ethics*. Lewiston: Edwin Mellon Press.
Benner P (1984) *From Novice to Expert*. Mento Park: Addison-Wesley.
Benson J (1983) Who is the autonomous man? *Philosophy*, Vol. 58, pp 5–17.
Brykczyńska G (1990) The gift of an organ. *Paediatric Nursing*, Vol. 2, October, p 12.
Brykczyńska G (1992) Caring – a dying art? In M Jolley and

G Brykczyńska (eds) *Nursing Care: The Challenge to Change*. London: Edward Arnold.

Burr S (1987) Quality of care – is it measurable? In *Cost and Quality in Child Health*, Conference Proceedings. London: King's Fund Centre.

Callahan D (1984) Autonomy: a moral good, not a moral obsession. *The Hastings Center Report*, No. 14, October, pp 40–2.

Central Health Services Council (1959) *The Welfare of Children in Hospitals: Report of the committee* (Chairman H Platt). London: HMSO.

Committee on Child Health Services (1976) *Fit for the Future*, 2 vols. (Chairman S D M Court). London: HMSO.

Cooper A and Harpin V (1991) *This is our Child: How parents experience the medical world*. Oxford: Oxford University Press.

Department of Health (1991a) *The Children Act 1989: An introductory guide for the NHS*. London: DoH.

Department of Health (1991b) *Welfare of Children and Young People in Hospital*. London: HMSO.

European Court of Human Rights (1986) *European Commission on Human Rights, decision as to admissibility of application*, No. 10929/84 (*Jan Neilson v Denmark*).

Fries C S (1989) The ethical issues of transplanting organs from anencephalic newborns. *The American Journal of Maternal Child Nursing*, **14**(6), pp 412–14.

Gaylin W (1987) In the beginning: helpless and dependent. In W Gaylin et al. *Doing Good: The Limits of Benevolence*. New York: Pantheon Books.

Gillick v West Norfolk and Wisbech AHA, 1985, 3 A11 ER 373.

HM Government (1989) Human Transplantation Bill. London: HMSO.

Huizinga J (1949) *Homo Ludens*. London: Routledge and Kegan Paul.

Hutchinson S (1990) Responsible subversion: A study of rule bending among nurses. *Scholarly Inquiry for Nursing Practice*, **4**(1), pp 13–17.

Hutt R (1983) *Sick Children's Nurses: A study for the Department of Health and Social Security of the career patterns of RSCNs*. Brighton: Institute of Manpower Studies.

Korczak J (1988) *King Matt the First*. New York City: Farrar Strauss and Giroux.

Lifton B J (1988) *The King of Children*. London: Pan Books.

Matthews E (1992) The ethics of rationing. In *Philosophy and Health Care*. Aldershot: Avebury.

Meadows R (1987) Children's services: The problems and prospects of rationalisation. In *Cost and Quality in Child Health*, Conference Proceedings. London: King's Fund Centre.

Milne A A (1989a) *When we were very young*. London: Methuen Children's Books.

Milne A A (1989b) *Now we are six*. London: Methuen Children's Books.

Milne A A (1989c) *House at Pooh Corner*. London: Methuen Children's Books.

National Association for the Welfare of Children in Hospital (1992) *Reducing the Stress of Operation Day*. London: NAWCH.

Rawls J (1971) *A Theory of Justice*. Cambridge, Mass.: Harvard University Press.

RCN (1988) *Specialties in Nursing*. London: RCN.

RCN (1992) *Paediatric Nursing – A philosophy of care*. Issues in Nursing and Health. London: RCN.

Robertson J (1958) *Young Children in Hospital*. London: Tavistock Publications.

Thorne R (1991) *Just for the day: Children admitted to hospital for day treatment*. London: NAWCH.

UNICEF, UK (1989) *Information sheet No. 8: A new charter for children* (3/88). London: UNICEF.

United Nations (1989) *Convention on the Rights of the Child*, Adopted by the General Assembly of the United Nations in 1990. London: HMSO. (CM 1990/1 1668.)

Further Reading

Brykczyńska G (ed.) (1989) *Ethics in Paediatric Nursing*. London: Chapman and Hall.

Brykczyńska G (1989) Informed consent. *Paediatric Nursing*, Vol. 1, July, pp 6–8.

CHAPTER 2

Care of the Elderly

Terry Chandler

Care of the elderly is often pushed to the margins, consciously or unconsciously. Yet, as the author of this chapter shows, the potential for the carers in this field is tremendous.

Problems of old age are legion. Problems in the care of the elderly arise at every turn, owing to lack of resources of almost every kind. The ethical problems for carers are therefore just as acute and as heartrending as in every other sector of care. This chapter challenges readers to look at some of these problems.

I don't feel my age – so my old age is not something that in itself can teach me anything. What does teach me something is the attitude of others towards me. Old age is an aspect of me that others feel. They look at me and say 'that old codger' and they make themselves pleasant because I will die soon and they are respectful. My old age is in other people.

Jean-Paul Sartre, age 80 years

Introduction

Nurses working in the care of the elderly, whatever the physical setting may be, are faced with many situations which are ethical in nature. The purpose of this chapter is to explore some of the issues they may be faced with, or indeed have experienced.

Nurses have a moral obligation to respect the individual patient's or client's wishes and the right to do whatever he or she thinks is correct. Nurses have a commitment to take care of patients. But the care provided by nurses in the interests of patients may in certain circumstances be opposed to the wishes of the patients. Often in the course of daily work, situations arise in which the wishes of the patients are not viewed as being of paramount importance and the actions determined by the professional carers are agreed to by the patient simply because the professional is deemed to know best, and the patient complies with those wishes.

Whoever we are, we are all subject to a greater or lesser degree of stereotyping in our expected patterns of behaviour. For instance, how often have we heard elderly people being berated for behaving in a manner which is perceived as being inappropriate. But inappropriate for whom? The individual? Or the observer? The individual has the right to dress or behave as he or she sees fit, providing, of course, that the behaviour is socially permiss-

ible. What Sartre says about old age being felt by others in this sort of instance would seem to be correct.

Elderly people are a very special group with a wealth of experience that the younger ones among us have yet to encounter. Some of these experiences we will probably never have, since our society has changed so radically, and some of the problems facing us as carers – and the elderly themselves – have not been experienced before. We are in a learning situation together. But by pooling our resources, we can learn how to deal with some problem areas.

Some of the situations facing us as nurses are not new, but we have not been able to reach solutions which are satisfactory to everyone. Perhaps this is a little too much to ask since the whole issue of values and beliefs is personal and the likelihood of all nurses agreeing on all aspects of care is very slight indeed.

Patients, whatever their age, are vulnerable. This vulnerability may be as a result of an altered health state. Many elderly people on admission are 'labelled' according to the perceptions of the nursing staff. For instance, many elderly people are considered to be confused and as such are often not given the courtesy of a detailed explanation of their treatment, because as far as the nurses are concerned, the patients' understanding is limited. On the other hand, patients may be too inhibited to ask for information and accept without question the decisions of the health-care professionals. This situation is not unique to the elderly, but can be found in any health-care setting.

The vulnerability of the elderly coming into hospital, perhaps for the first time, can be exacerbated by the attitude of the staff. Staff may assume that patients do not want to know more, or that they do not wish to be involved in the decisions being made for their care. Alternatively, staff may decide not to give a patient more information because in their opinion the patient would not understand it. By withholding information nurses are doing the patient an injustice. They presume that what they are doing is in the patient's interest. But do nurses have the right to make such judgements? Situations like these are common because what nurses do is done out of concern for the patients' welfare. However, most people have some understanding of their illness and therefore if explanations are not given in language patients can understand, all sorts of sinister thoughts may enter their heads and so increase the patients' anxiety or misunderstanding of what is going to happen to them.

These broad issues will be examined in more depth in this chapter, but first some terms and measurements of care will be detailed.

Ethical terms

In simple terms, ethics is concerned with the meaning of right and wrong, good and bad, responsibility and duty. Each one of us has a set of values and beliefs, or rules, by which we live. These are the result of the influence of many factors, including family, education, culture and religion, and these form the basis on which people decide that certain actions are right or wrong, and what we ought to do or indeed have the right to do.

Within every moral code, the idea of wantonly taking human life is considered wrong and to save life is generally held to be right.

If we have the time to think through a problem and weigh the consequences, the decision-making process is made easier, not in terms of the decision, but in terms of choosing the action that is most appropriate. However, in nursing and health care, decisions have quite often to be made on the spot and sometimes the actions available lead us into a 'Catch-22' situation, where whatever course of action is decided on, it may prove 'harmful'. When faced with moral dilemmas, most of us tend to act instinctively in accordance with our own values. Many believe that there is a natural law governing ethics on which moral codes are based. The proponents of natural law challenge the right to interfere with the 'natural' course of events by trying to control them. Another way of choosing the course of action is to take the utilitarian approach and ascertain whether the end justifies the means, and leads to the greatest happiness for the greatest number.

There is no easy way to determine what is right or wrong or good or bad, or indeed whether we have a duty to do anything at all. In nursing there are standards of acceptable practice, which are determined by the statutory body and also recommendations by the professional bodies, which help in the determination of these very difficult areas of nursing practice.

Measuring Long-term care

Long-term care was defined by the Scottish Home and Health Department (1975) as the care provided to people who have been categorised as critical–interval dependent for a period of more than 28 days.

For those people who are unlikely to be discharged from care, the present policy advocated by the government is the provision of small units close to family and friends. The objective of this type of unit is to provide a homely atmosphere and promote individuality, personal dignity and the expression of personal preference.

No doubt there are establishments which do just that. Sadly, this is not the case in all places where elderly people are cared for on a long-term basis, as the media have often highlighted. One of the factors that is frequently put forward in defence of appalling situations is the lack of resources and the cost implications of ensuring that adequate provision is being made. Can we justify the cost of a service that provides for the care and welfare of people?

If care is approached appropriately, then the quality of patients' lives could always be improved, even with the resources provided.

Perhaps it is the attitudes and values of the nurses working in these settings that need to be questioned. Perhaps they are in the wrong job. Perhaps those who do wish to ensure quality provision view their lot as hopeless and the system as unbearable. It could be that fear is the key, and that if nurses 'rock the boat' they believe that their jobs will be in jeopardy. Professional carers have to decide whether or not they can let the status quo continue or whether they tackle the problem and try to improve the lot of those for whom they care.

One of the major problems in determining resource allocation in the health service is that it is not always possible to compare separate health-care regimes, whose outcome measures are based on different criteria. Quality Adjusted Life Years (QALYs) were designed so that the outcome of health services could be measured in a single index over time (Williams 1985).

QALYs

The Quality Adjusted Life Years measure is a combination of expected life years gained from health-care procedures together with a judgement about the quality of expected life years gained. In this way the life years gained are subject to a quality adjustment – hence the term.

> The essence of a QALY is that it takes a year of healthy life expectancy to be worth 1, but regards a year of unhealthy

life expectancy as worth less than 1. Its precise value is lower the worse the quality of life of the unhealthy person (which is what the 'quality adjusted' bit is all about).

If being dead is worth 0, it is, in principle, possible for a QALY to be negative, i.e. for the quality of someone's life to be judged worse than being dead.

The general idea is that a beneficial health care activity is one that generates a positive amount of QALYs and that an efficient health care activity is one where the cost per QALY is as low as it can be. A high priority health care activity is one where the cost per QALY is low, and a low priority activity is one where cost per QALY is high. (Williams 1985)

The basic assumptions of QALYs in the United Kingdom were that improvements would be made in life expectancy and reductions in disability and distress would be achieved (ibid.). In 1986 The University of York produced a discussion paper on the cost per QALY data as an input to the decision-making process determining resource allocation in one Regional Health Authority (Gudrex 1986). Earlier studies by Neugarten, Harringhurst and Tobin (1961) and Luker (1979) identified a reliable measure of satisfaction with quality of life. But a consensus does not exist about the different ways of measuring the quality of life of elderly people in long-term care.

QALYs are based on the belief that given the choice, a person would prefer a shorter healthier life to a longer period of survival in a state of severe discomfort and disability.

There are two possible ways of employing QALYs. The first is to use them in determining which health-care activities to employ for particular patients and which procedure(s) to use to treat particular conditions. This gives plausibility to QALYs. The other way is to determine which group of patients to treat. This is really indefensible. Williams (1985) suggests that 'one year of healthy life is of equal value no matter who gets it' and that each person's valuations 'have equal weight'. The person determines the value of life to him or her; when an individual's life is cut short, this is a wrong done to that individual. If, however, the health service continues to concern itself with improving efficiency, then this second way may become the more influential, and the one with the most far-reaching consequences.

One could say that QALYs are implicitly biased against age. The saving of a young life, all things being equal, is likely to produce more QALYs than saving older people. If health authorities are concerned with producing more and more QALYs, and competing with each other for QALYs, the elderly will necessarily come off worst.

QALYs dictate a preference for people who have 'more life expectancy to be gained from treatment' rather than those who simply have 'more life expectancy'. Life-saving interventions, such as the timely administration of antibiotics, are likely to gain more life expectancy for the young than for the old. Other groups (such as handicapped people or those with specific illnesses) who could be discriminated against could fare as poorly as the elderly, if statistics dictate discrimination in the allocation of resources.

It is important to note that QALYs make no distinctions between types of treatment. Treating a young person with eczema may be more QALY-efficient than resuscitating an elderly person.

Those of us who dislike any kind of hierarchical system and would welcome a society without different classes of people are likely to question decisions which imply that one person's life is more worth saving than another. The whole social climate is affected when groups of people are not confident that their interests will be given equal weight with others. Expectation of life is always relevant to a choice of saving life.

Gould (1975) argued that in a crisis most of us would

prefer to save a 'normal' person rather than someone in the final stages of a terminal illness, or rescue a young person rather than someone in their nineties. If we subscribe to the philosophy that all beings are equal, it is the number of life years saved rather than the number of lives saved which is of greater importance.

In the name of justice, as well as efficiency, we have got to adopt new methods of medical accounting. One assesses the relative importance of threats to health in terms of the loss of life-years they cause. Calculations are based upon the assumption that all who survive their first perilous year ought then to live on to the age of 70 (any extra years are a bonus). In Denmark, for example, there are 50,000 deaths a year, but only 20,000 among citizens in the 1–70 bracket. These are the ones that count. The annual number of life-years lost in this group totals 264,000. Of these, 80,000 are lost because of accidents and suicides, 40,000 because of coronary heart disease, and 20,000 are due to lung disease. On the basis of these figures, a large proportion of the 'health' budget ought to be spent on preventing accidents and suicides and a lesser but still substantial amount on attempting to prevent and cure heart and lung disease. Much less would be spent on cancer, which is predominantly a disease of the latter half of life, and which therefore contributes relatively little to the total sum of life-years lost. Little would go towards providing kidney machines, and even less towards treating haemophiliacs. No money at all would be available for trying to prolong the life of a sick old man of 82 (Gould 1975, pp 220–1).

It has been suggested that those with children or other dependants should be given priority over the childless or friendless in the allocation of health care. It has also been noted that some believe that children are entitled to priority because they have not had what older people have had, namely the attainment of adulthood. Consideration of this raises the question of the validity of age-related criteria in the distribution of health-care resources.

It has been argued that QALYs are not an appropriate way of measuring the quality of life of elderly people requiring long-term care, mainly because they are based on a scale that uses disability and distress as its main indicator (Rosser and Harris, 1965). QALYs have never been studied in people over the age of 60 years (Donaldson et al. 1988). Others have highlighted the dangers of relying on a single measure of the quality of life, and question a purely economic approach (Baldwin et al. 1990).

Yet elderly people constitute a group that is increasing in size, while other groups are at present declining in numbers. Furthermore the majority of elderly people continue to live their lives with minimal intervention.

'If death is the unequivocal and permanent end of our existence, the question arises whether it is a bad thing to die' (Nagel 1979). In the context of this chapter, the question is, however, how this dying is done.

Specific issues relating to the elderly

Elderly people often neglect themselves. This does not in itself constitute an ethical problem. What does make it an ethical problem is the person's refusal of help, or the opinion, attitudes or beliefs of others which determine the ethical context in which the professional carer has to work and make decisions. Often an elderly person's refusal of care is due to the fact that they believe that help is too late for them, possibly as a result of what has been said to them in the past, comments like 'What else do you expect at your age?'

Self-neglect could be a result of depression in the elderly person, leaving a feeling of unworthiness or guilt, and a wish to die. Elderly people are often fatalistic in their outlook. But not all elderly people who express a wish to die can be diagnosed as depressed. It may be that their lives have become so intolerable that death would be a happy release. In this situation a person may accept help passively in the hope that death comes soon so that he or she is not a burden to relatives or carers. It is important to appreciate the strength of these beliefs and not simply to attribute them to ignorance.

Religious beliefs are also very important. Many elderly people view their problems as the will of God. They often see their lot as a punishment for some sin committed in the past and may become so preoccupied with their guilt that all offers of help are rejected.

Elderly people living in the community are subject to all the stresses caused by the environment which threaten their ability to maintain their independence. There are special groups who are, according to Norman (1985) subject to the 'triple jeopardy' of age, discrimination and lack of access to services.

Many of the problems associated with the elderly are that the decisions made about their future are based on situations which arise as an emergency. Emergency action is needed to deal with many situations whatever the age of the individual, and as such we do what is necessary to preserve life. But in the case of some elderly people, the action taken, for example the removal to hospital, becomes the permanent answer to the problem without taking into consideration any alternatives. It could be that the elderly person gives up a home to live with a relative in the short term without considering the long-term prospects, or, as in the following case study, moves into a nursing home.

- Mr Davies was admitted to a nursing home following an acute psychotic episode while staying with his daughter. He had been diagnosed some years earlier as suffering from Parkinson's disease, but managed very well on his own in his ground-floor flat. However, two years earlier he had been diagnosed as suffering from dementia. Since then he had deteriorated and become very forgetful.

Because of the family circumstances, consideration for long-
term care had been given. Mr Davies' daughter had
discussed this with the GP and nurses and was told that the
likelihood of her father's being able to care for himself in
the future was remote. She decided to sell his flat in order
to be able to keep him in a nearby nursing home where she
would be able to visit him regularly. After a period of time
in the home Mr Davies expressed a wish to return to his flat.

The implications for all concerned in this situation, which
is not uncommon in the care of the elderly, are that in
attempting to ensure the well-being of Mr Davies other
problems have been caused and ethical issues are raised.
Maintaining elderly people in their own home carries a
certain amount of risk. In determining the well-being of
the person all these risks have to be taken into consideration.

It is all well and good when the persons concerned can
appreciate the dangers of living alone, but what about the
situation where someone is genuinely incapable of making
such a decision and a decision has to be made on their
behalf? Some of the professionals involved in this decision-
making process are reluctant to do this and justify their
decisions as those needed to protect the person rather than
viewing it as forcing someone to do something they do
not want to do.

Looking at the situation objectively, one can see that
anything that is done to protect a person involves some
form of positive deprivation. Even the use of cotsides or
chairs is ostensibly to protect the patient. One can take
the example of not letting elderly people bath on their
own for fear of their injuring themselves.

In the main elderly people have been conditioned to
respect authority, and in care settings the professional carer
represents authority. Elderly people will often accept professional advice without question. In all decisions of this
nature we would do well to remember to judge as we

would wish others to judge for us were we to be in a similar situation.

Giving information

A situation that nurses often face in caring for elderly people is that of diagnosis and who has to be informed. For instance, a patient who does not want his or her relatives to know the diagnosis or prognosis, or indeed vice versa, puts nurses in a very difficult position.

To respect the patients' wishes and rights would, on the surface, appear to be the right course of action to take. But do relatives not have a right to know? It is easy to say that patients' wishes have to be respected and adhered to, but should nurses necessarily abide by this rule? How can we deal with the problem? Obviously it is not our role gratuitously to divulge information, but have we a role in discussing with the patient and trying to convince the patient that relatives need to know? What about fielding the questions relatives ask? Do you deny all knowledge? Hardly. The relatives will think that you don't care about the patient if you appear not to know what is wrong! Do you couch your answer in such a way that relatives are left confused about what is happening to the patient? Or do you hint that there may be something 'serious' wrong with the patient? By not explaining what is wrong, you may cause more anxiety and stress.

In short, do you tell the truth or not? Social life itself relies on truth and honesty. However, this principle is probably the most difficult to maintain. Trust forms a basis for relationships and therefore involves other people directly. To live by the old maxim 'the truth, the whole truth and nothing but the truth' is impossible. A nursing ethic related to truth-telling and honesty is inextricably linked to confidentiality and also to consent.

The relationships nurses build with their patients are based on this fundamental principle, in an attempt to promote a climate of openness. In order that this situation may be achieved, nurse and patient need to co-operate by sharing and involving, and accepting each other's vulnerability. In all relationships there has to be give and take.

The UKCC Code of Professional Conduct (1992) is unequivocal about the professional conduct of the nurse: 'Each registered nurse, midwife and health visitor shall . . . protect all confidential information concerning patients and clients obtained in the course of professional practice and make disclosures only with consent.' The UKCC Advisory Paper *Confidentiality* (1987) implies that *trust* is the focal point of the relationship.

Based on the assumption that telling the truth is good and that this should be the norm in nursing practice, why is it that so often we don't? Downie and Calman (1987, p. 152) suggest that you should ask yourself:

> Are there circumstances where you would not tell the truth?
> Are there circumstances when you would lie?
> Are there circumstances when you would force the truth
> on the patient (for his own good)?

Seedhouse (1988) stresses that as truth-telling is such an important principle of human conduct, strong justification is required if the principle is to be overridden.

Truth-telling and honesty are grounded in the principles of the value of life and of freedom, which means that people should be afforded the respect of truthfulness.

Consent

The notion that patients have a right to give or withhold consent to treatment is relatively new historically. In order to make an informed choice the patient requires information, and that information has to be both meaningful and understood by the patient. There are certain groups of patients or clients who are genuinely incapable of making informed and educated choices and decisions. In these situations a third party may be involved to act as advocate for the patient. This may be the next of kin or a lawfully appointed person who has taken control of the patient's affairs. 'If the patient is considered unable to give valid consent, it is considered good practice to discuss any proposed treatment with the next of kin.' (NHS Management Executive 1990)

Consent to treatment is reasonably straightforward if the proposed treatment is life-saving or essential to the well-being of the patient. 'It becomes more of an ethical issue when the treatment is not aimed specifically at improving the client/patient's health, nor is it life saving' (Rumbold 1991).

Wandering behaviour

One of the problems of working with the elderly mentally ill is the constant wandering some of them engage in. This can be very provoking and nurses often find difficulty in observing patients constantly. Some doors may be locked. Is it right that elderly persons should be 'imprisoned' in wards like this? The reasons given are normally that it is for the protection of the patient; but is it ethically right? This is a situation where the greatest good for all has to be considered. You could argue that locking a door is an infringement on the person's rights, but then you may come up against a situation where patients wander out of the area and into greater danger.

There are many reasons for wandering behaviour. It may be defined as 'purposeful', that is the patient is acting out established patterns of behaviour which are implanted

in the long-term memory. It could be their former occu-
pation, or a ritual which they carried out daily, and despite
the surroundings, continue to do. As an example, a person
may have kept chickens and every night at 5pm fed them.
Every night now he goes out 'to feed the chickens'. What
do you do? Do you try to stop the behaviour by telling
him that the chickens have been sold? Is it absolutely
necessary to try to change this behaviour?

The behaviour could be linked with bereavement in
which the patient is searching for a spouse.

Unpurposeful wandering always presents a management
problem. More often than not the lack of adequate
resources makes the problem worse: there are not enough
nurses to implement the necessary care activities. Do you
feel that as a nurse you have an obligation or a duty to
attempt to secure adequate resources? If so, how would
you go about it?

With regard to the locked door, is it ethically tenable
to restrict a person's movements like this? If you consider
the Utilitarian principle of the greatest good for the greatest number, then you could argue that what is happening
is to the benefit of the majority. But is it?

Restraints

There are other forms of restraint which are used, for
instance chairs which have tables attached to prevent the
individual from getting out, or the use of cot sides on
the beds to prevent patients getting out of bed. Medication
is another form of restraint. How do you feel about the
use of restraint of any description?

It is often important to use medication in an attempt
to control behaviour which is disruptive, in order that
nursing care can be effective. However, its effect can lead
to the opposite and patients may become so uncommuni-

cative as a result of medication that nursing intervention is impossible. It can also be very distressing for relatives to see a normally active person reduced to inactivity. In some situations one can argue that the use of medication is necessary for the safety of the patient, and that to withhold its use may increase the distress of both patient and relatives.

The question is, do the patients genuinely consent to the regime of medication or is it an imposed regime? Is this regime ethically correct in your opinion?

Often in the care of elderly mentally ill persons, their behaviour is attributed to their mental state, when their behaviour could be a result of physical discomfort, or that newly admitted persons wander because they do not know where they are. Imposition of restrictions increases the patients' dependence and reduces independence and autonomy. 'Every human being of adult years and sound mind has a right to determine what shall be done with his own body . . . ' (Cordoza 1914).

Smoking

Is it right – morally and ethically – to stop an elderly person from smoking? What about the patient of advanced years diagnosed as having respiratory disease? We are all too well aware of the dangers of smoking and the harm it can do, not only to the smoker, but to others.

In some situations you may be able to present the patient with these facts. Or your hospital may have a no-smoking policy. How far is this an infringement on civil liberty? On the one hand, you know the harm that the patient is subjecting himself or herself to, but as a nurse do you have the right to make the decision for the patient? Is it right to impose a no-smoking rule on someone who may have been smoking for over sixty years?

What about people who are terminally ill as a result of smoking? Is insisting that they stop smoking going to affect the prognosis, or is it going to increase their stress? Have we the right to impose our values on patients in these circumstances?

There are many issues surrounding smoking. It is not an easy problem to deal with, but then no problem is. When you take account of the wishes of the smokers to continue smoking, you also have to be cognisant of the fact that there are other people involved; their health and welfare have also to be considered. The non-smokers in a care environment are also being put at risk.

In keeping with government policy many hospitals are either totally smoke-free areas or are in the process of becoming smoke-free. Certainly, it is easier to impose such rules in areas where patients are likely to be for short-term care, but what about the areas where people are nursed on a long-term basis and that area is essentially their home? Can we justifiably restrict their activities, or do we make concessions? There are programmes which could be set up to help people to stop smoking, but what if they do not wish to do so? What about the dangers of people seemingly going along with the policy, but actually ignoring it by smoking in secret in places where the risks are increased with fire hazards?

One could debate *ad infinitum* the rights and wrongs of smoking and not come to any conclusions. Perhaps these issues can only be raised, but never totally solved.

Diet

Most elderly people have eaten what they want, when they want and how they want. When they come into hospital, they are subject to the menus available from the catering department. Nutrition experts organise well-balanced diets to ensure that individuals get all the essential elements. But is that what an elderly person wants?

One of the problems of diets is the way in which the food arrives. It may be totally unrecognisable to the patient. Our menus have seen the inclusion of items such as pizzas and other 'exotic' foods. We have also seen the introduction of wholemeal bread, skimmed and semi-skimmed milk, butter substitutes, etc. In today's climate where the population at large is becoming more health-conscious and more selective about what they eat, the choice is theirs to make whether they change the dietary habits of a lifetime or not.

In hospitals these decisions are taken on behalf of the patients, and although patients are given the opportunity to select their meals, the choices available may not be what they would have been shopping for. It is very difficult, in fact almost impossible, in these circumstances to cater for each individual's choice but it does restrict the individual freedom of choice.

Catering for the needs of the minority in cases of dietary requirements, for example vegetarians and special diets required for religious reasons, does not prove to be so problematic. Perhaps we ought to consider this provision in terms of offering the opportunity for the elderly person to enjoy a meal of their choice?

Fast foods are now a way of life for the young, but to the elderly a burger on a bun, however enjoyable you may think it is, is not what they are used to. Do we as nurses impose what we know to be a more healthy approach to diet? Do we have the right to do so?

The choices available today in most hospitals and residential homes where elderly people are cared for are, in the main, excellent. What is lacking is a little imagination. It is fair to say that the food presented today is much better than a few years ago when elderly people were served mince, mashed potatoes and over-cooked vegetables together with tea containing milk and sugar.

Property and finances

Care of the very frail or mentally ill elderly people brings with it the inevitability of ethical or legal dilemmas concerning their property and the appropriate management of their finances. You may have come across situations where relatives have taken charge of the person's pension, but you know that the individual receives nothing or very little of it. This aspect of care of the elderly is a thorny problem indeed. How do you feel about this type of exploitation? Is there anything we as nurses can do?

What about the situation where the patient may wish to change a will in favour of the hospital or care setting in which he or she is now being cared for? How do we ensure that suspicions of coercion are avoided? There are no easy answers.

It is vital that the financial affairs of patients are treated in the strictest confidence and that any financial negotiations are undertaken by the relevant authority and not by the nursing staff, and that in all matters regarding property professional advice is sought.

The wish to return home

How do we as nurses deal with the patient who repeatedly expresses a wish to return home? In many instances the prognosis is so poor that a return home is not a viable option. What do you say in this situation? This calls into play the principle of truth-telling and honesty. How 'economical with the truth' should nurses be? Is it right that all hope of ever returning home is denied the patients when

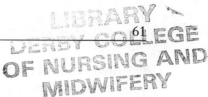

this might be the one thing that keeps them going? A lot depends on the relationship you have with the patient and how honest you are.

Compulsory removal from home

The other side of this problem is the admission to hospital of people who want to stay at home. 'Putting father in a home' is a very difficult decision for relatives to make. Nurses often condemn this choice and believe that the relative should take over the care of the mother or father for the remainder of their life. But this is unreasonable. The relative needs all the support the care staff can give. This also raises the question of admission against the will of any individuals when their ability to care for themselves is impaired. This situation highlights a duty of care by the professionals but highlights also one of the most difficult ethical decisions, namely the compulsory removal from home of a person, as the following case study shows.

- Mr Carlisle was a gentleman in every sense of the word. Financially he was secure. Mr Carlisle's mother had died some years ago leaving him a very large detached house which he and his wife, who died nine years ago, rented out.

  About four years ago, when Mr Carlisle was 65, he sold his family home and moved into the ground floor of his mother's house where he lived quite comfortably until a year ago, when his last tenant vacated his room, leaving Mr Carlisle on his own. Although not a particularly sociable man, Mr Carlisle would pass the time of day with neighbours. However, lately his conversations with his neighbour, Mrs York, had become slightly odd; he had started expressing fears of being persecuted. Mrs York, who had a passing acquaintance with Mr Carlisle's son, who visited his father occasionally, mentioned this to him, and as a result his son requested a visit by the GP. When the doctor visited Mr Carlisle, he noticed that the house was untidy and dirty. An appointment was then made for a psychiatrist to visit.

  Mr Carlisle told the psychiatrist that some of the people around him were persecuting him and sending spirits into his house through the gas pipes. He took the psychiatrist into one of the rooms on the ground floor to show him where the spirits were coming in.

  Following a full assessment, the psychiatrist suggested that Mr Carlisle come into hospital. Mr Carlisle was not willing to do that but expressed a willingness to take medication. The psychiatrist gave him a prescription and arranged for the community psychiatric nurse (CPN) to visit and monitor him closely.

  Following one of the visits by the CPN, Mr Carlisle's behaviour became more bizarre. This resulted in his being admitted to hospital under a compulsory section of the Mental Health Act 1983.

While in hospital Mr Carlisle responded well and he was discharged. Within a week he had refused to let the CPN into the house and subsequently had a relapse. The GP and the psychiatrist were in no doubt that compulsory admission was required. The psychiatric social worker assigned to his case did not agree and again Mr Carlisle was persuaded to take medication at home.

Shortly after the visit of the psychiatric social worker, Mr Carlisle again refused to grant entry into his house and his behaviour became worse; so much so that the CPN was very worried about him and was fearful of trying to gain entry into the house. She contacted the GP, the psychiatrist and the social worker involved, and a compulsory admission to hospital was enforced. But Mr Carlisle's son was totally opposed to the admission.

In the decision to take someone who is at risk into hospital or residential care, the duty of care has to be set against the rights and freedom of the individual. Together with the duty of care the individual's rights have to be weighed against the rights and needs of the other people involved, i.e. the relatives. The question of right or wrong in this situation – as in others – is not simple. It is more than likely that the professionals will be of one opinion, and relatives and friends of another. The assessment of risk is often subjective rather than objective, because of pressure exerted by both sides. This situation poses the question: Who determines what is normal and what is not in relation to the individual?

You have probably come up against patient behaviour which you deem to be abnormal, when in fact it may just be an extension or exaggeration of the person's normal behaviour. You may consider that the patient requires treatment, but many elderly people receive treatment because their behaviour is a problem to others rather than to themselves.

A major issue here is obtaining a true measure of

informed consent as this is very time-consuming. 'During episodes of illness the autonomy of patients should be maintained throughout treatment . . . and active partici-pation of patients in their own treatment should be facili-tated by open and sensitive discussion' (RCN 1976).

'Do Not Resuscitate' orders

Rumour has it that at one time in some hospitals people over 65 had on their identification bands the letters 'NTBR', indicating that in the event of collapse they were 'not to be resuscitated'. It takes little imagination to see what effect this could have on a patient's morale, should he or she discover what the letters stand for. What do you tell a patient who asks what the letters mean?

'Do not resuscitate' instructions raise a number of ethical questions for nurses (see chapter 3, *Aspects of Nursing Care*). There is the question of who decides. In some instances it is the doctor who makes the decision as a result of assessing the expected quality of life of the patient.

There may be situations where not to resuscitate some-one is the kindest act you as a nurse can take. But imposing a blanket policy could prove to be very dangerous and not take account of the person's individuality or possible qual-ity of life. There are situations where you may believe that to prolong a person's life by implementing life-saving measures is unacceptable since all you are doing is prolong-ing suffering.

But not all suffering is physical. Some elderly people appear to be in abject misery as a result of a mental illness, or are so far out of touch with reality that it is difficult to assess their true feelings. You may have nursed someone suffering from dementia and whose links with reality seemed to be totally lost. What do you think about instruc-tions not to resuscitate them? From our point of view the patient's quality of life may appear to be poor, but how do we really know?

Bandman and Bandman (1990) argue that it should be the patient who decides, not the professional:

> Playing God by deciding who has the required quality of life and who therefore lives or dies also reveals a serious moral pitfall of arbitrarily abridging the equal rights of individuals to decide whether to live or die.

In allowing patients to exert their rights to decide, nurses are not relieved of moral conflicts.

The UKCC Code of Conduct (1992) does not help the nurse to resolve the conflicts either, but emphasises them. Clauses 1 and 2 require that the nurse, midwife and health visitor:

1 Act always in such a manner as to promote and safeguard the interests and well-being of patients and clients.
2 Ensure that no action or omission on your part, or within your sphere of responsibility, is detrimental to the interests, condition or safety of patients and clients.

Not to resuscitate, even if in accordance with the wishes of the patient, could be seen as 'not promoting their well-being' and as being 'detrimental to their interests.'

Clause 7 requires that nurses, midwives and health visitors:

> recognise and respect the uniqueness and dignity of each patient and client, and respond to their need for care, irrespective of their ethnic origin, religious beliefs, personal attributes, the nature of their health problems or any other factor.

Should nurses not accept the patients' right to decide not to be resuscitated, they could be seen as violating clause 7.

In a survey of hospitals in the United Kingdom, Aarons and Beeching (1991) found that in many of the hospitals taking part in the survey no clear guidelines existed. They also highlighted the fact that 'elective decisions not to resuscitate are not clearly communicated to nurses'. At the conclusion of their survey they advocated 'more discussion of patients' suitability for resuscitation between doctors, nurses, patients and patients' relatives'.

What do you consider to be the criteria on which to base such a decision? How would you feel if the policy-makers in the areas in which you work wanted to introduce a policy like this? What options do you as a nurse have in this situation?

1 You could accept it without question.
2 You could try and change it.
3 You could refuse totally to conform with the policy.
4 You could ignore it until the situation arises and then refuse to comply.

Perhaps you may wish to ignore the policy in the hope that the situation will not arise while you are on duty, or you may consider the professionalism of your role as a carer and consider what is expected of you as a nurse in terms of your professional duty. If you accept this policy, ask yourself why. Is it that you feel that as an employee this is what is expected of you? Perhaps you may think that contractual obligations dictate your acceptance. Or you may consider this to be the less complicated option to take. You may link acceptance to the possibility that you may never come up against this situation, so your personal thoughts and values may not be brought into question. But this is somewhat unrealistic.

You may have thought that the correct course of action is to try to change the policy. Are you in a position to do that and how would you set about it? To change a policy of this nature may be what your conscience dictates and you may consider it to be what is expected of you as a caring professional. Trying to change a policy is a long and difficult road to follow and not one to be entered upon lightly, but this can be a most fulfilling exercise.

You could, of course, simply refuse to comply, but in doing so you are confronting authority and you are probably aware of nurses who have refused to comply with certain policy statements and are now branded as troublemakers. In situations like this, time is seldom taken to seek the views and reasons for non-compliance, even though the reasons may be highly pertinent. To take the option of non-compliance by paying lip-service to the policy, but in the event of being faced with the situation ignoring the stated policy, is essentially dishonest.

Euthanasia

The subject of euthanasia has been debated over a long period of time and attempts at legislation go back to the 1930s. The debate ranges across political, legal, ethical and religious divides. This can be seen in many of the professional publications and the national press. Euthanasia is usually discussed in terms of either 'active' or 'passive' relating to the methods adopted (see chapter 4, *Ethics – Aspects of Nursing Care*).

The term passive euthanasia concerns the permitting of death in circumstances such as terminal illness or suffering in which the doctor uses his or her skill and expertise to ensure that death is as painless as possible. In the case of an elderly, terminally-ill patient, should the doctor increase the dosage of the analgesic to relieve pain, then the dose may be so big that it brings about death. However, the law does not classify this as 'mercy killing' since the doctor is not actually 'killing' the patient.

Active euthanasia (i.e. killing without the patient's permission) is concerned with an act that results in the painless death of a person.

The distinction between active and passive euthanasia is thought to be crucial for medical ethics.

To begin with a familiar type of situation, a patient who is dying of incurable cancer of the throat is in terrible pain, which can no longer be satisfactorily alleviated. He is certain to die within a few days, even if the present treatment is continued, but he does not want to go on living for those days since the pain is unbearable. So he asks the doctor for an end to it, and his family joins in the request.
   Suppose the doctor agrees to withhold treatment, as the conventional doctrine says he may. The justification for his doing so is that the patient is in terrible agony, and since he is going to die anyway, it would be wrong to prolong his suffering needlessly. But now notice this. If one simply withholds treatment, it may take the patient longer to die, and so he may suffer more than he would if more direct action were taken and a lethal injection given. This fact provides strong reason for thinking that, once the initial decision not to prolong his agony has been made, active euthanasia is actually preferable to passive euthanasia, rather than the reverse.' (Rachels 1975)

The arguments surrounding euthanasia give rise to many dilemmas of a moral, religious and ethical nature. In the Hippocratic Oath there are contradictions. The doctor promises to 'relieve suffering' yet also to 'prolong and protect life'. Nursing elderly patients, and indeed any patients in similar circumstances, can be harrowing for all concerned in their care.

Nurses often find themselves in situations where both sides of the argument can be seen. Increasing the dosage of a drug could hasten death, but to withhold the increased dosage would result in more distress and discomfort for the patient, and indeed for the nurse who often feels quite helpless in this situation. How do you reconcile the dilemma? What about the wishes of the patient? How can you comply with wishes of patients when it goes against all that you value and believe in?

There have been attempts at legalising euthanasia in England and Wales but to date all proposals have been defeated.

Some countries such as Sweden have legalised passive euthanasia. The Swiss penal code (1957) distinguished between killing with bad intentions (murder) and good intentions (mercy killing). In the United States the California National Death Act 1976 allows patients to instruct their doctors not to keep them alive by 'extraordinary means' if they are dying. In this instance 'extraordinary' could mean attaching patients to respirators (*The Economist* 1976).

What about the patient who is expressing his or her right to die? How do you feel about this? What do you do about it? Clearly, if nurses were to be involved in the administration of euthanasia, were it to be legalised, then this would raise issues in relation to the UKCC Code of Professional Conduct (1992) and might indeed highlight some contradictions between the clauses.

One aspect of the nurse's role in relation to euthanasia which would be questioned is that of patient advocate. How would nurses fulfil this particular aspect of their role in the context of euthanasia? Advocacy is concerned with protecting the rights of patients and ensuring that patients can exert those rights. It is also concerned with the interests of patients. Nurses acting as patient advocates would then be promoting and acting in the patients' best interests. One problem which may be raised is in relation to who decides what is in the best interests of the patient. The patient may take the view that it is in his or her best interests that life should be ended. The nurse may take the opposite view. Can the nurse therefore be a true advocate of the patient?

The Code of Professional Conduct (UKCC 1992) emphasises the primacy of the patients' well-being and interests, but offers little in the way of clarification as to how to resolve the conflicts that arise from a difference of view.

The case for euthanasia depends on our understanding and interpretation of the terms 'well-being' and 'interests of the patient'. Nurses could find themselves in a situation where it could be argued that death may be preferable 'in the interests of the patient', but maintaining life may not promote the patient's 'well-being'.

The nurses' rights and duties

So far in this chapter we have looked at the rights of the patient and the duties of the nurse towards the patient. But what about the rights of the nurse? Does becoming a nurse infringe on our rights as a person? Yes, becoming a nurse does impinge on our rights as a person. When we become nurses, regardless of which sphere of nursing activity we choose to work in, we accept certain duties which are part of the role of the nurse. One such duty is that, as nurses, we must ensure that no harm befalls our patients. There are times when the nurse's rights as a person conflict with the expectations of professional duty.

There are situations in which the nurse has the right to make conscientious objections to taking part in situations or treatments, and this has been recognised by the UKCC Code of Professional Conduct (1992): '(8) As a nurse . . . you must . . . report to an appropriate person or authority . . . any conscientious objections which may be relevant to your professional practice.'

Where do nurses stand if they feel that patients are being mistreated? The term 'conscientious objection' means different things to different people. In this context it relates to the patients' right to informed consent and the nurses' right to refuse to give treatments. It also covers such issues as carrying out unnecessary treatments, or taking part in mental or physical abuse.

Certain treatments carried out in the care of the elderly (and indeed in other spheres of nursing) are controversial and cause concern for some nurses, for example electro-convulsive therapy (ECT). Some elderly people admitted with depression may be subjected to this form of treatment. It is fair to say that in some instances recovery has been remarkable, but not in all. Many nurses feel that this form of treatment is barbaric and unnecessary when there are other forms of interventions which could be employed. What do you feel about ECT? If the patient is able to make a decision that is based on a full explanation, which he or she understands, do nurses have the right to object to take part in ECT as the treatment of choice? If the patient is not in a position to give informed consent, this is a different matter.

What about other situations where the patient is not in a position to speak out for himself or herself? There have been a number of cases where maltreatment of patients has been reported by nurses, or where nurses have spoken out about the lack of resources available to ensure adequate nursing care.

As a professional you are in a position to make up your own mind on what action you think is correct. It is not easy to stand alone, but as has been demonstrated in the past, one voice, if loud enough, will attract the attention of others who feel as strongly about the problems of ensuring the best possible care for the elderly patient while considering their best interests.

Nurses working in areas where elderly mentally ill people are cared for often find this type of nursing exhausting, both mentally and physically. In some instances the areas in which elderly mentally ill people are cared for are less than acceptable given the resources. Many nurses avoid working in areas like this for a number of reasons, including the view that this type of nursing is custodial and nothing can be done for the individual. Over the past few years attitudes have changed and more nurses are rising to the challenge of improving the lot of the elderly mentally ill.

This chapter has been a short overview of some of the issues which face nurses working in the care of the elderly, and indeed other areas of nursing practice. Perhaps it has given you food for thought and the opportunity to reflect on your own values and beliefs.

References

Aarons E J and Beeching N J (1991) Survey of 'Do not resuscitate' orders in district general hospitals. *British Medical Journal*, **303** (14), December, pp 1504–6.

Baldwin S, Godfrey C and Propper C (Eds) (1990) *Quality of Life: perspectives & policies*. London: Routledge & Kegan Paul.

Bandman E L and Bandman B (1990) *Nursing Ethics Through the Life Span*. New Jersey: Prentice-Hall, 2nd edition.

Cordoza B N (1914) '*Schloendorf v New York Hospital*'. In Gorovitz S et al. (eds) (1976) *Moral Problems in Medicine*. Englewood Cliffs, N.J.: Prentice-Hall.

Donaldson C, Atkinson A, Bond J and Wright K (1988) QALY's and long-term care for elderly people in the UK. Scales for assessment of quality of life. *Age & Ageing*, **17**(b), pp 379–87.

Downie R and Calman K (1987) *Healthy Respect: Ethics in health care*. London: Faber & Faber.

Economist (1976) The California National Death Act, 9 October.

Gould D (1975) Some lives cost too dear. *New Statesman*, 21 November.

Gudrex C (1986) *QALY's and their Use by the Health Service*. Discussion Paper no. 20. University of York, Centre for Health Education.

Luker K A (1979) Measuring life satisfaction in an elderly female population. *Journal of Advanced Nursing*, **4**, pp 503–11.

Mental Health Act (1983). London: HMSO.

Nagel T (1979) Moral Questions. In P Singer (ed.) (1990) Applied Ethics. *Oxford Readings in Philosophy.* Oxford: Oxford University Press.

Neugarten B L, Harringhurst R J and Tobin S S (1961) The measurement of life satisfaction. *Journal of Gerontology*, **16**, pp 134–43.

NHS Management Executive (1990) *A Guide to Consent for Examination or Treatment.* London: NHS Management Executive.

Norman A (1985) *Triple Jeopardy – Growing Old in a Second Homeland.* London: Centre for Policy on Ageing.

Rachels J (1975) Active & passive euthanasia. In P Singer (ed.) (1990) Applied Ethics. *Oxford Readings in Philosophy.* Oxford: Oxford University Press.

Rosser C and Harris C (1965) *Family & Social Change.* London: Routledge & Kegan Paul.

Royal College of Nursing (1976) *RCN Code of Professional Conduct – A Discussion Document.* London: RCN.

Rumbold G (1991) *Ethics in Nursing and Midwifery Practice.* London: Distance Learning Centre, South Bank Polytechnic.

Scottish Home and Health Department (1975) *The Measurement of Need in Old People.* Scottish Health Service Pamphlet No. 34. Edinburgh: Scottish Home and Health Department.

Seedhouse D (1988) *Ethics: The Heart of Health Care.* Chichester: John Wiley.

UKCC (1987) *Confidentiality: An Elaboration of Clause 9 of the Second Edition of the UKCC's Code of Professional Conduct for the Nurse, Midwife and Health Visitor.* London: UKCC.

UKCC (1992) *Code of Professional Conduct for the Nurse, Midwife and Health Visitor,* 3rd edition. London: UKCC.

Williams A (1985) Economics of coronary artery bypass grafting. *British Medical Journal*, **291**, pp 326–9.

CHAPTER 3

Care of People with HIV and AIDS

Ben Thomas and **Stephen Firn**

The advent and spread of HIV (Human Immuno-deficiency Virus) and AIDS (Acquired Immune Deficiency Syndrome) has been a challenge to society from the beginning. The authors deal with these challenges from many different aspects, including that of infected health-care workers. They tackle the issues which HIV and AIDS have highlighted in all care: confidentiality, informed consent and research. The much discussed topic of living wills is also given space in this chapter, which is written with sensitivity and authority.

Introduction

Caring for people with HIV infection and AIDS inevitably raises many ethical issues for nurses. Many of the questions and dilemmas that are discussed in this chapter are not unique to the field of HIV and AIDS. Nevertheless, the very nature of the syndrome is such that it highlights many aspects of care which nurses have traditionally found difficult. These include issues surrounding sexuality, death and dying, and behaviours deemed deviant in society, such as drug misuse.

HIV and AIDS are identified together as one of the priority areas in the Department of Health's *The Health of the Nation* (1991) as AIDS is potentially the greatest threat to public health this century. To protect against HIV and AIDS, the government has developed a five-part compre-

hensive strategy, co-ordinated across all government departments. This covers prevention, monitoring, surveillance and research; care and support; social, legal and ethical issues; and international co-operation.

AIDS is a relatively new syndrome and many nurses have very limited experience in caring for people infected with HIV. In addition, no other public health issue in modern times has been surrounded by such fears and prejudice (Miller and Bor 1989). Thus it is perhaps not surprising that many nurses caring for people with HIV are still practising in an atmosphere of ignorance and confusion (Akinsanya and Rouse 1991). This has tended to influence and distort debates on issues such as the nurse's duty to care and the nurse's role in ensuring that confidentiality is maintained and informed consent always obtained. Such issues may be further complicated by the fact that HIV is transmissible and may cause fatal illness.

Boyd (1989) and Fowler and Chaney (1989) have addressed ethical concerns related to HIV in terms of three major moral principles. These are (1) beneficence or non-maleficence, (2) autonomy and (3) justice. The principle of beneficence requires that good should be done by health-care workers, while non-maleficence reminds us that if it is not possible to do good, we should at least prevent any harm coming to patients. The principle of autonomy indicates respect for a patient's wishes and interests, and this is most commonly practised through informed consent. The principle of justice demands that the needs of all patients are fairly judged and nursing care evenly distributed. It has been argued that if all these principles are followed, then an ethical problem no longer exists (Boyd 1989).

Unfortunately, in the emotive and contentious area of HIV and AIDS, a number of situations may arise where it is not possible to satisfy all three principles and where nurses may disagree on what constitutes ethical practice. Tschudin (1992) suggests that an ethical dilemma arises when no clear solution exists and nurses are forced to choose between two or more not wholly satisfactory alternatives.

When faced with ethical dilemmas a number of authors have argued that nurses should remember that caring is central to their role.

While technical knowledge embedded in nursing procedures is important, it is the more intuitive skills and personal attributes involved in looking after the interests of another human being that are the essence of nursing (Morrison and Burnard 1991). Thus, an ethical paradigm in nursing requires an understanding of the moral principles described above with an ability to establish authentic caring relationships with each patient, whatever his or her lifestyle, background or illness. 'Practical ethics is about marrying the ability to deliberate and come to good decisions while continuing to be involved with other people's life events.' (Brown et al. 1992)

Whenever possible, this chapter will make reference to actual care examples to illuminate the ethical dilemmas under discussion. This is in an attempt to ensure that the human dimension is not lost from these debates.

Confidentiality

The UKCC *Confidentiality* document (1987) states that as a general principle patients have a fundamental right to information about them being kept private and secure unless they authorise disclosure to a third party. This is to prevent personal, social or legal repercussions as a result of any disclosure. This relates to the principle of non-maleficence or doing no harm.

The ways in which people with HIV infection and AIDS have experienced rejection and discrimination have been well documented (Aggleton and Homans 1988). This has led to people being shunned by friends, family and lovers, dismissed from their jobs, and evicted from their homes because it has become known that they are infected with HIV. It can therefore be seen that disclosure of someone's HIV status can have a catastrophic effect on that person's well-being, and many would argue that this should never be done without the person's permission.

Nevertheless, an individual does not have a statutory right to confidentiality and the UKCC acknowledges that certain exceptions may exist. However, the UKCC (1987) clearly states that the only justification for a breach of confidentiality is if the nurse believes it to be in the patient's best interests or in the public interest. Nurses are further advised that they must be prepared to justify their actions in a civil court if an individual seeks recompense through the law.

Health care staff: who needs to know?

Nurses work as part of a multi-disciplinary care team. If a patient is HIV-positive this information will usually be available to staff providing direct patient care. This is because the diagnosis is likely to be relevant to the patient's overall care plan because of its potential psychological, physical and social effects. However, the size and composition of the direct care team will vary. Decisions will need to be taken about which staff need to know the diagnosis. For instance, does an occupational therapist carrying out an assessment need to know the person's HIV status? What about an agency nurse who may only be working one shift on the ward? While it is preferable that decisions to inform such members of staff, or indeed third parties such as general practitioners, are multi-disciplinary decisions, a nurse may have to make rapid decisions on these questions. In such situations it is always best to ask the patient. If this is not possible, then the nurse must decide what the patient would want, based on the relationship he or she has established. As part of the nursing assessment of a person with HIV, it may be prudent to explore the patient's feelings about which members of staff are to be informed of the diagnosis.

Some nurses feel that because HIV is transmissible and can cause fatal illnesses, any member of staff who comes into contact with the patient should be informed of the diagnosis, regardless of whether they are involved in direct patient care. This may include portering and domestic staff. However, the infection control procedures required for the safe care of a person with HIV are the same as those required for the safe care of *all* patients, and should therefore be practised by all staff in all situations

(Pyne 1991). With these issues in mind, it would be very difficult to justify such a breach of confidentiality as being in the patient's best interests or as being in the public good.

Because of the intimate nature of the relationships nurses often forge with patients, they may be more likely than other members of staff to receive information which the patient considers confidential. This is demonstrated by the following example.

- A patient was being investigated in a neurosurgical unit for peripheral neuropathy and motor dysfunction. Repeated tests had failed to find an organic cause for his condition. One day the patient called his primary nurse and said he had something to tell her which he had never told anyone else. He then confided that he had been diagnosed as HIV-positive the previous year but had not experienced any physical symptoms. The nurse recognised that his current condition was almost certainly due to the neuropathological effects of the virus and stressed the importance of informing the rest of the care team so that appropriate treatment and care could be initiated. The patient only agreed after the nurse convinced him that the disclosure of this information would not lead to hostility from the care staff and that his relatives and work colleagues would not be informed of the diagnosis.

If the patient had not agreed to the nurse sharing this information with the direct care team she would have faced an ethical dilemma. Should she inform her colleagues in order that appropriate treatment and care, albeit not curative, could commence; or should she respect the patient's autonomy? Which would be in the patient's best interest?

Perhaps one way of avoiding such dilemmas is for nurses to advise patients that they work as part of a team and they share information with their colleagues involved in the patient's direct care. This allows the patient to choose what information to divulge. Certainly alarm bells should ring for a nurse if a patient says: 'I have something to tell you which I don't want anyone else to know.'

Should sexual partners, relatives and significant others be informed of the diagnosis?

Many nurses would state that the simple answer to this question is that only those partners or relatives whom the patient wants to be informed should be told the diagnosis. This is a very good general principle since it respects the patient's autonomy and precludes the possibility of harm coming to the patient through unauthorised disclosure of their HIV status.

However, the UKCC *Confidentiality* (1987) document does state that nurses are entitled to breach confidentiality if it is required by a court of law or if they believe disclosure is in the public interest. Many people would argue that because HIV is transmissible and can lead to fatal illnesses, health-care professionals have a duty to inform those who are at risk of acquiring HIV from the patient, or who may already have been infected. This would clearly apply to current sexual partners (unless safer sex practices were being stringently observed). Recent improvements in prophylaxis and treatment have led to increased life expectancies for people with AIDS. Not telling relevant persons that they had been exposed to HIV could be seen as denying them these potential benefits to their health.

It may also be argued that informing sexual partners of people with HIV has potential public health benefits since there is evidence that education and prevention campaigns have not been successful in persuading the majority of people to change their HIV risk behaviours. An HIV-positive diagnosis may be more likely to induce behaviour change incorporating safer sexual practices.

There are a number of counter-arguments against

informing partners without consent. The consequences of a breach of confidentiality are potentially greater for HIV than for other illnesses, including other sexually transmitted diseases. This is because of the rejection and discrimination that some people with the virus have experienced in their public and private lives (Aggleton and Homans 1988).

Another forceful argument is that if patients felt that health-care staff would be likely to divulge their HIV status without seeking permission, they might be deterred from taking an HIV antibody test. Even if people knew their status, they might be reluctant to tell health-care staff for fear of disclosure and its consequences. This could have the effect of driving the disease underground, preventing people coming forward for treatment, and resulting in an even greater spread of the virus. Proponents of this view maintain that the only way to minimise the spread of HIV is through education, prevention initiatives, and promoting tolerance and compassion towards those infected. They argue that revealing HIV diagnoses without informed consent is more likely to increase the public health threat from AIDS.

The current situation in the United Kingdom regarding partner notification by genito-urinary medicine (GUM) clinics is somewhat confused. Some have established HIV contact tracing programmes, while others do not follow this practice. Those clinics that do attempt to trace partners usually do this by asking people before they take an HIV antibody test to answer questions about sexual partners. They are informed that if the result is positive, attempts will be made to contact these partners. While the ethics of this practice are debatable, given many of the issues discussed above, at least the patient is aware of what will happen if the result is positive, can decide whether to proceed with the test, and may have the opportunity to go to another clinic which does not trace partners.

The types of situation and dilemma confronting nurses working in other settings are likely to be of a different nature. For example, in one situation a nurse was caring for a man with AIDS who was shortly to have an arranged marriage. His future wife and her family did not know the patient's HIV status. Understandably, the nurse was keen to respect the patient's autonomy and preserve their caring relationship. However, she also felt that the future wife had a right to be made aware of the potential risks to her health and that of any offspring. In such instances, how does a nurse resolve his or her commitment to maintaining confidentiality while also acting to safeguard the well-being of other citizens? Issues such as these must be considered carefully within the direct care team and decisions made only after exploring the individual circumstances in each case. Nurses have an active role to play in this decision-making process, particularly as they often have the closest professional relationships with the patient and significant others.

Health advisers, counsellors and mental health nurses with experience in this area have a vital role to play in helping patients to explore the risks of unprotected sexual intercourse and the possible consequences of not informing sexual partners. In addition, they can help the patient to clarify their fears about informing partners, what they think might happen, and if appropriate, decide how and when to tell partners (Miller and Bor 1989).

Some people with AIDS find it particularly difficult to reveal their diagnosis to significant others, such as their parents, since this may also involve disclosing aspects of their lifestyle, such as drug use, homosexuality or prostitution. Patients in this situation are often concerned that their parents will reject them or that they will be very distressed by the news and it is kinder to pretend that they have some other illness. This can mean that a patient may have a number of visitors at one time, some of whom are aware of the diagnosis and others who are not. Nurses need to discuss this possibility with patients, and one nurse, such as the primary nurse, should be allocated as the only person who discusses the actual diagnosis with visitors. However, in order to avoid breaching confidentiality by accident, nurses need to be prepared to respond in a caring and compassionate manner to distressed visitors who want to know what is wrong with their loved one. Nurses may also have a central part in helping and supporting patients before, during and after the process of telling a loved one about their diagnosis.

Informed Consent

Informed consent is derived from the principle of autonomy and respects a person's right to make choices about his or her own well-being. Barker and Baldwin (1991) assert that consent is the giving of permission to someone to do something which that person would not have the right to do without such permission. 'Informed' means that a person must be able to make a decision after receiving and understanding sufficient information to enable him or her to make an educated and responsible choice. This will include information such as the nature and purpose of an intervention, any potential hazards and other care or treatment options. Consent must also be given voluntarily and without coercion or undue pressure. As such, consent is not simply a legal and ethical requirement; it is also a requirement at the heart of the caring relationship.

It can be argued that all nursing interventions and interactions impinge on a person's privacy and hence require consent. However, in practice it is simply not possible to give all the information necessary to enable a patient to make a fully informed decision about every treatment and all conceivable options. Consent is therefore frequently implied, especially in procedures where there is little likelihood of causing harm, such as the measuring of vital signs.

When caring for a person affected by HIV, the principles of informed consent are no different from those relevant to the care of any patient. However, it is generally true to say that the people who have been most affected by HIV have been relatively young, articulate and adept at asserting their rights. In addition, many people with HIV are very knowledgeable about the latest research and drug trials and are aware of treatment alternatives. This has meant that nurses have found that many patients with HIV have insisted on being actively involved in decisions about their care to a greater extent than other client groups. This has reinforced the need for nurses in this area to keep up-to-date with current research and practice, and to be open and receptive to questions about their care.

Perhaps the greatest ethical debate has centred on the HIV antibody test (Firn 1991). The availability of this test means that people can be identified as having being infected with the virus even if they have not experienced any symptoms of HIV disease. However, the test is for antibodies to HIV and these can take three months to develop. This means that people may show HIV-negative if they have been tested during this 'window period'.

Should informed consent always be obtained before taking blood for an HIV antibody test? After all, blood is frequently taken for routine screening, during which the type of tests which are conducted are rarely discussed in detail with the patient.

Many people have argued that there are significant differences between routine tests and tests for HIV which mean that an HIV test cannot be treated like many other blood tests, and that pre-test counselling should always be offered to people considering this test. For instance, it is widely acknowledged that a positive HIV antibody test result may precipitate significant psychological trauma. Not only must the person come to terms with the fact he or she is infected with a virus that causes life-threatening illnesses, but may also face many of the negative psycho-social consequences related to the unique stigma attached to the virus (Miller and Bor 1989). Research has suggested that the absence of a thorough discussion of the meaning and potential consequences of the test result leads to a lower psychological preparedness for the result (Mansson 1990). The result may also have an effect on a person's insurance or mortgage applications and a further important consideration is that although improved forms of treatment are helping to ameliorate symptoms and improve the quality of life for infected persons, there is still no cure or vaccine available for HIV (Medical Defence Union 1989). As a result of thinking through these issues during pre-test counselling, many people have decided that it is not in their best interests to undertake an HIV antibody test. Thus, while a number of benefits may accrue to some people from finding out their HIV status, nurses risk causing harm if they participate in unconsented testing for HIV, particularly if the result is positive. The UKCC (1992b) has advised nurses that they may risk criminal charges of assault, civil action for damages and being reported for professional misconduct if they participate in the taking of blood for unconsented HIV antibody testing.

However, the UKCC (ibid.) also acknowledges that:

> there are rare and exceptional circumstances when unconsented testing may legitimately occur. These must be able to be justified as in the interests of the particular patient at the operative time, and for no other reason, and only where it is not possible to obtain consent.

Thus, as when considering other ethical dilemmas, nurses are urged always to try to act in the best interests of individual patients in each situation and wherever possible avoid doing harm.

The UKCC does not give examples of the situations in which 'unconsented testing may legitimately occur'. However, it is likely that this refers to situations where people are unable or not competent to give consent, perhaps because they are unconscious or experiencing a mental illness, but for whom an HIV test may be in the best interests. Pratt (1991) suggests one scenario in which an unconscious patient is admitted with no next of kin. The person's symptoms indicate an HIV-related aetiology which may benefit from anti-retroviral therapy if the diagnosis is confirmed. Another situation could be a person with unexplained cognitive impairment who is not competent to give informed consent, and whose symptoms are consistent with HIV-related central nervous system disease. If an HIV diagnosis could be confirmed the person may benefit from anti-retroviral therapy. In such cases it may be possible to reconcile unconsented testing, with the potential for harm that this entails, with beneficence. However, nurses should be aware that unconsented HIV antibody tests will not necessarily be appropriate or ethically justifiable for any patient with an unexplained mental health problem. Nurses must continually exercise their professional judgement in each situation to assess the validity of such action.

Some professional bodies have argued that in certain situations the autonomy of the patient is secondary to the health-care professionals' right to know a patient's HIV status. They draw on the principle of justice to argue that when health-care professionals are exposed to risk, they have a right to know the extent of that risk. For instance, the Royal College of Surgeons (1990) has stated that patients who are considered to be at 'high risk' of HIV may be tested without consent if a member of the operating team sustains an injury. The aim of this is to inform the health-care workers whether or not they have come into contact with the virus. Although this would clearly not meet the UKCC criteria for proceeding with an unconsented test, since the test would be carried out in the primary interests of the health-care worker, many nurses do support this proposal as this quote from a theatre nurse demonstrates: 'I think that if a nurse has been injured, testing should be allowed without the patient's consent' (Lyall 1991).

The potential deleterious effects of such a policy on a patient's well-being have already been discussed. It is also important to remember that it may take three months from infection for HIV antibodies to develop. During this period the test result will be negative, indicating the limited value of the test in such situations. It is also a moot point that if theatre staff consider they have the right to know a patient's HIV status, should not patients also have the right to know the status of those who are taking part in the operation?

Testing without consent has also been advocated to protect people in direct contact with a person with HIV infection.

- A man was admitted to a psychiatric hospital in a highly distressed and agitated condition. He claimed he had AIDS and was biting his arms and spitting blood at staff and patients. The medical staff suggested that he should be tested for HIV. However, the only way to prevent the risk of infection to staff would be for the patient to cease the self-harming behaviour.

The universal protection control precautions that are required in such situations are no different from those required for the same care of any patients, whether or not they are known to be carrying an infectious agent. The staff do not need to know the patient's HIV status in order to care safely and fairly, and it is therefore difficult to justify abandoning the usual requirement of consent.

Unlinked anonymous HIV antibody testing

The UKCC has also supported the programme of unlinked anonymous testing (UKCC 1992b). This programme uses blood taken for other purposes in areas such as genito-urinary medicine clinics and antenatal clinics. A residue of the specimen is rendered anonymous and is tested for HIV. While informed consent is not sought before testing the blood, the local research ethics committee must have given approval for the programme in each case and the patient is given access to explanatory literature as well as the opportunity to discuss the study, and can object to the use of the blood for this purpose. The justification for this programme is based on the utilitarian principle of the greatest good for the greatest number (Gillespie 1992); that is, it is considered in the public interest to obtain the most accurate epidemiological information possible in order to provide and target resources to meet identified need.

In 1991 The Royal College of Nursing Congress voted overwhelmingly to urge the government to ban the anony-mous testing programme. This was because some studies were publishing data such as the hospital where the tests were conducted, and the sex, ethnic origin and HIV risk group of those people found to be HIV-positive. Congress felt that the patient's anonymity was not being sufficiently protected because of the inclusion of such data, and this could cause distress to individuals who had attended these hospitals.

Pyne (1991) has stated that the UKCC will continually review the anonymous testing prevalence programme to ensure that research protocols are not breached. In particular, nurses are requested to ensure that patients in areas where the programme is taking place have access to written and verbal information which they are able to understand; and that any patients who object to participation in the study will not experience any discrimination or detriment to their care.

Duty to Care

The image of nurses being compassionate and non-judgemental carers was well and truly threatened with the advent of HIV and AIDS. This was clearly evident from the results of a number of attitude surveys, which showed that many nurses were no different from the general public in their fears and prejudices towards people with HIV and AIDS. Reports of nurses refusing to care for people with AIDS were common. The confusion and anxiety generated at the time manifested itself in extreme measures carried out by some nurses to protect themselves from the minimal occupational health risks involved. This over-reaction included patients being isolated in side-rooms, not because they might be at risk from others but because they were thought to be a risk to staff and other patients. They were given disposable sheets, gowns, crockery and cutlery and were further humiliated by practices such as the marking of blood samples with a pink triangle or other distinguishing features which added to their segregation.

That was in the mid- to late-1980s and many nurses have since gained an enormous amount of knowledge and experience in caring for people with HIV and AIDS. Despite this knowledge and insight, a significant number of nurses believe that they should have the right to refuse to care for people with AIDS (Akinsanya and Rouse 1991; Bond et al. 1990). This reluctance continues to be related to fears of infection and notions of patients being deviant and undeserving of care.

Refusal to care for patients on the grounds of fear of infection is a disproportionate reaction to the likelihood of becoming infected. Fowler and Chaney (1989) suggest that by the very nature of their work nurses must accept a level of exposure to disease which exceeds that expected by the general population. This is not to say that nurses should either be exposed or expose themselves to unnecessary risk, but rather that they should take proper precautions to ensure that risk of infection is minimised. The basic procedures to be followed with regard to preventing infection in relation to HIV are commonly known as 'universal infection control precautions'. These are based on the general principle that the number of people who are asymptomatically infected with HIV is unknown and it is not possible to guess who is or who is not infected just by looking at a person or basing judgements on their lifestyle. It would also be impractical to subject all patients to an infection screen and, even if screened, those who have not yet seroconverted to HIV would remain undetected; therefore nurses should take reasonable precautions against exposure to blood and body fluids from all patients all the time, regardless of knowledge of their HIV status. Not only does this approach minimise the risk of infection, but it also helps to maintain confidentiality about infected patients. The introduction of these guidelines has encouraged nurses to adopt safer working practices, for example in the handling and disposal of sharps, such as not resheathing used needles.

Information relating to HIV and AIDS is constantly changing. Nevertheless nurses have an obligation to keep up-to-date as specified by clause 3 of the 'Code of Professional Conduct for the Nurse, Midwife and Health Visitor' with its requirement to improve knowledge and competence (UKCC 1992a). Providing nurses with the known facts about the modes of transmission of HIV is obviously not sufficient to allay their anxieties since many nurses remain fearful of becoming infected with HIV through patient contact. As well as the dissemination of written information and didactic teaching, other methods of training have experimented with structured exercises and group discussions. Through this work it has become clearly identified that nurses not only need support in the form of policies and procedures in relation to infection control, but that they also require clinical supervision and other methods of staff support.

Objecting to care on the grounds of a patient's lifestyle is unacceptable practice amongst caring professionals. Clause 7 of the Code of Professional Conduct points out that nurses should recognise and respect the uniqueness and dignity of each patient and client and respond to their need for care, irrespective of their ethnic origin, religious beliefs, personal attributes, the nature of their health problem or any other factor. Fowler and Chaney (1989) suggest that lifestyle should be considered a patient attribute which is to be used to individualise the nursing care plan, not to deny it. The UKCC states that those nurses who refuse to care for patients with HIV or AIDS could be charged with serious professional misconduct (UKCC 1992b). Apart from the threat of disciplinary measures, discrimination by nurses against those whose lifestyles do not conform to society generally has been confronted mainly by a range of educational programmes. Many of these programmes provide nurses with an opportunity to explore their own personal agendas, fears and anxieties about a number of issues directly related to AIDS including sex, sexuality, homosexuality, drugs and death. Of course, these issues are not peculiar to nursing people with AIDS. However, it was in trying to provide care to people with AIDS that these deficiencies in nurse training became more apparent. For example, either sexuality was not addressed

at all in the curriculum or if mentioned it was restricted
to theoretical input related to anatomy, physiology and
altered bodily function (Thomas 1990).

Present training is aimed not merely at enabling the
acquisition of knowledge, but providing an opportunity
for participants to explore their attitudes, to transfer existing skills and to develop some new ones. Didactic teaching
has given way to much more participatory techniques such
as group discussion, structured exercises, role play and
psychodrama. In encouraging participants to examine their
attitudes, many courses involve people with HIV infection
and AIDS on course teaching. A number of course-leaders
believe that contact with people with AIDS is a major
factor in attitudinal shift. Cranfield and Dixon (1990) suggest, however, that some trainers question whether the
incorporation of people with AIDS into training courses
is not a form of exploitation.

The short duration of these courses means that at best
they are only able to begin to raise awareness. Unfortunately, there is an assumption by many managers and
indeed some nurses that attending courses such as the
English National Board's 934 course in 'Care and Management of People with HIV and AIDS' will equip them
with the 'right' attitude and the necessary skills to look
after people with HIV and AIDS. Without denying the
benefits which can be gained by attending such courses,
they are only an introduction and should be followed
up with more in-depth training as and when required.
Unfortunately, many nurses are not able to afford such
courses and managers are reluctant to allow them time off
in an already overstretched health service.

Nurses who work with patients who have HIV or AIDS
often experience psychological stress (Ross and Seager
1988). Despite the risk of burn-out associated with long-
term contact with individuals with HIV infection and

AIDS and their families, many nurses do not have clinical supervision or formal support systems built into their day-to-day work. Managers have an ethical obligation to provide the necessary means for such support to take place in order to protect the well-being of nurses and to reduce the risk of burn-out.

Employees with HIV Infection

All health-care workers pose a potential infection risk to patients. As far as HIV transmission is concerned, its incidence is extremely rare in this country, but, despite this, reported cases of HIV-infected health-care workers cause excited fears among the general public and even among health-care professionals themselves. In the early days of the epidemic, panic resulted in prejudice by employers, and many health authorities reacted unjustifiably by suspending or dismissing HIV-positive health-care workers on the grounds that they were an unacceptable infection threat to patients. A more humane and constructive response is now adopted by most health authorities faced with such a predicament. Nevertheless, the anxiety spread by the media's amplification of such incidents is demonstrated by the call for compulsory HIV testing of all health-care workers, and accusations that the government and the medical profession gloss over the risk of patients acquiring HIV infection in hospital (Sadler 1992).

According to the recommendations made by the Expert Advisory Group on AIDS (1991), any policy which compels defined groups of individuals to be screened for HIV infection would be counterproductive. They suggest that such a policy is discriminatory, interferes with an individual's rights, and may deter those who are most in need of education and counselling from seeking advice. The Expert Advisory Group therefore concludes that in the

light of current knowledge, routine screening of health-care workers undertaking invasive procedures, as a measure to protect patients from infection, is not considered justified. Until recently some health authorities did in fact carry out pre-employment screening. This usually consisted of a health declaration questionnaire, which was often aimed at trying to assess 'at risk' groups and risk behaviours, but more generally enquired about any HIV antibody tests already taken. Apart from the inappropriateness of pre-employment screening, such a process does raise all sorts of moral and ethical questions, particularly from an equal opportunities perspective. When confronted about pre-screening questionnaires, many hospitals and health authorities have argued that they were acting in the best interests of applicants, since knowledge of their HIV status would enable counselling, support and appropriate advice regarding work assignment to be available.

The UKCC's (1992b) statement on AIDS and HIV infection recognises that all practitioners pose a potential infection risk and emphasises that all nurses must ensure that high standards of clinical practice are maintained to safeguard and protect patients. Nurses who believe that they may have been exposed to HIV infection should not automatically assume that this will lead to termination of employment or suspension from work. In most circumstances, providing high standards of clinical practice are carried out, the nurse is not an infection risk to patients. The Expert Advisory Group on AIDS recommends that nurses who are infected and engage in invasive surgical procedures must obtain advice from their occupational health department. They may need to change or modify their work practices. But each nurse should be assessed on an individual basis. They may need to be assigned to a different clinical area for protection from acquiring opportunistic infections.

It is important that employers promote a climate of trust and support. Nurses must be assured that their status and rights as employees will be safeguarded, including their right to confidentiality. Apart from stating the nurse's level of fitness to carry out his or her work, no other information is required to be shared by the occupational health department and managers. Every effort should be made to support nurses who are HIV-infected. This may involve emotional support, such as counselling, or practical assistance, such as arranging suitable employment and providing retraining opportunities.

Advance directives and living wills

Advance directives refer to instructions made by patients wishing to have some control over what happens to them during the course of their illness, up to and including their death. Their popularity in the medical context has come about as a result of new and advanced treatments and technologies, which have increased the possibility of sustaining terminally ill patients. Usually such statements are made either by the persons themselves, in which case it is referred to as a living will, or by the persons naming someone else whom they would want consulted and who would make decisions on their behalf. Such a person is referred to as a proxy or as acting under an 'enduring power of attorney for health care'. A proxy is consulted by the doctor when a decision about life-sustaining treatment is required and the patient is unable to communicate his or her wishes.

As in so many other controversial areas, HIV and AIDS have raised awareness of advance directives and brought the subject to the forefront of ethical debate. This has been prompted by a combination of forces. First, our current knowledge and treatment remain limited and we cannot prevent either the fatality of AIDS or the devastating effects of neuropsychiatric syndromes caused by HIV. Second, user empowerment and patient choice have become prominent themes in contemporary health care. Nowhere has this been more pronounced than in the area of HIV and AIDS. This is evident from the proliferation of self-help groups, voluntary organisations and other alternative services which challenge existing orthodoxies. In addition, *The Patient's Charter* (DoH 1991) emphasises the needs, rights and wishes of the individual patient and reinforces the patient's right to be involved in decisions concerning care.

Often people with AIDS are aware of the possible outcomes of the syndrome and the medical treatment available and want to make their own decisions about what happens to them while they are still fit enough and competent to do so. Many countries, including the United States, Canada and Australia, have now introduced legislation and practices which support and regulate advance directives. While it is usually doctors who make the decisions in this country regarding life-sustaining care, it has become more common for nurses to participate in those decisions. Additionally, the concepts underpinning nursing practice include maintaining the patient's rights and dignity, respect for individual choice and maximising independence. With these in mind many nurses have expressed dissatisfaction with the ways decisions about life-sustaining treatment are currently managed in HIV care (Schlyter 1992). They complain that presently decisions are taken without any knowledge of, or reference to, the patient's wishes.

Schlyter's study examined the interest for advance directives and current procedures for decision-making about life-sustaining care and the potential role for advance directives in relation to HIV and AIDS. The results of the study suggest that the majority of people who took part are interested in the use of advance directives and stated that there should be more discussions about life-sustaining care between patient and doctor. Fifty-five out of 64 people with HIV and AIDS stated that they would consider writing a living will. Ten people with AIDS had discussed life-sustaining treatment with a doctor, but thirteen who had not, said they wished to do so. Many of the people who were HIV-positive but who had not developed AIDS also wanted to discuss life-sustaining care with their doctor. However, few of those who were either HIV-positive or who had AIDS would like to name a relative to take decisions about medical care for them.

Among the nurses interviewed in the study many were concerned about the lack of communication between patients and doctors over life-sustaining treatment. They thought that decisions all too often had to be taken without any indications of what the patient would have preferred. Many nurses stated that the main benefit from a living will is that it gives patients some control (or a better sense of control) over the treatment they will receive. However, many were worried about patients who, after having made a living will or designated someone else as proxy, might change their minds. Schlyter suggests that such concerns may be lessened if it is firmly understood that a living will is not a final document, but can be changed by the patient either orally or in writing, and that this applies to a proxy appointment. Additionally, living wills should be the basis of continuing discussions between patient and doctor.

In conclusion, Schlyter points out the need to raise awareness and to disseminate information about advance directives. She suggests that model forms should be provided in patient organisations, hospitals and clinics and that guidelines should be produced by official or professional bodies. Advance directives have a potential role to play in improving decision-making practices about life-sustaining treatment for people with HIV and AIDS. The present time seems appropriate for some formal measures, legal or extra-legal, to be considered in the United Kingdom.

Research

Medical interventions, particularly drugs and vaccines, have come to enjoy tremendous prestige in modern society. That expectations of a cure for HIV has not materialised during the past ten years has raised a number of ethical questions about scientific research generally, and more specifically about biomedical research into HIV and AIDS. Accusations have been made of personal suffering caused by mismanaged funds, scientific impotence and inadequate government responses. In line with the growing trend, many of these challenges have not only been made by patient advocates but by patients themselves. The trend towards patient empowerment, self-determination and a more questioning attitude towards professional practice and scientific research pre-dated AIDS; nevertheless this new wave of patient participation and decision-making has severely affected health professionals' competence and power.

Wachter (1991) suggests that the effect has been to energise the fight against AIDS with an urgency that has translated into expedited drug approvals, lower prices for medications and increased funding for AIDS research and care. Alternatively, many people argue that self-help groups and activists are doing more harm than good by alienating natural allies such as doctors and scientists and that they gain a disproportionate influence on health-care policy. Hawkes (1992) likens the AIDS activists in the United States to 'the lunatics taking over the asylum.' Such an analogy only demonstrates his lack of compassion and understanding for the mental health user movement in trying to empower patients and emphasise their right to information, choice and self-determination. Hawkes' naivety is also evident in his argument that the greatest danger posed by activists is that they will deliberately hamper the open-minded search for the truth about AIDS and HIV. Today, there are few people who would not argue that AIDS is a complex social and political phenomenon. AIDS research is inherently political, and to suggest that there is some neutral truth waiting to be discovered through scientific research is dogmatic and misleading.

Hawkes suggests that the advice given to patients by self-help groups may contradict that given by doctors and other professionals, particularly in relation to medication. This may lead to patients mixing and matching various drugs and failing to comply with the medication prescribed by doctors. Such behaviour makes it difficult to conduct controlled clinical trials of new drugs. While acknowledging the necessity for drug research, including the standard medical double-blind controlled trials and that such research is both costly and time-consuming, patients' consent to participate must always be obtained.

As far as possible they should be allowed to make their own decisions about their therapy. *The Patient's Charter* (DoH 1991) highlights that patients have a right to refuse to participate in teaching and research activities. Horton (1989) suggests that the ethics of human experimentation should always be governed by principles other than scientific merit alone.

The immorality of human experimentation without the consent of subjects has been highlighted in the recently publicised scandal of the syphilis experiment in Alabama, where 400 black men were left to die while the doctors who conducted the research not only misled patients about the disease but denied the men treatment (Smith 1992). The linchpin of the experiment was a nurse who throughout the project followed doctor's orders unequivocally. It was her role to persuade the men to take part in the study and to persuade the families of the deceased to donate the bodies for autopsy.

Today nurses are more fortunate than the nurse described in the syphilis experiment. The UKCC (1992b) provides advice in relation to AIDS research, particularly in respect of anonymous screening programmes. The UKCC states:

> any patient or client who objects to participation in the test programme should have his or her wishes respected fully and should not:
> (a) be discriminated against in any way;
> (b) be identified as being at higher risk than those who have not objected and
> (c) have required treatment withheld or suffer any other detriment.

Summary

This chapter has explored some of the ethical issues surrounding HIV and AIDS and the ways in which these articulate with nursing care. Many of these issues have created dilemmas for nurses and nursing for which there is no wholly right or wrong answer.

The emergence of the virus has reignited many debates around confidentiality. These centre principally on who has legitimate access to information about the patient and in what – if any – circumstances should a nurse consider breaching confidentiality in the public interest. The potential for harm resulting from a breach in confidentiality may be greater because of the ignorance, fear and prejudice that still surround the syndrome. This unique stigma, coupled with the knowledge that HIV can cause fatal illnesses and no cure is available, has contributed to an awareness of the potential psychological and social harm which may result from a positive HIV antibody test. This has forced many nurses to examine more closely what constitutes informed consent. More recently, the UKCC (1992b) has acknowledged that in exceptional circumstances unconsented testing may be justified in the patients' best interests. Nurses can and should play an integral role in making such judgements, advocating on behalf of the individual patient and always striving to utilise a caring ethic.

Nevertheless, a significant number of nurses continue to respond to people with AIDS in a negative and prejudicial manner. This has reopened debates about nurses' duty to care.

Should someone who is openly hostile to people infected with HIV be able to refuse to provide care? If not, should anyone be forced to care for a person with AIDS, and what are the consequences of this? A lively ethical debate has taken place around who needs to be informed when a practising nurse is HIV-positive or has AIDS. For instance, some people have argued that patients have a right to know when a nurse is HIV-positive. However, if universal infection control precautions are followed, there is a very low risk of an infected nurse transmitting the virus to a patient. Nevertheless, nurses who take part in invasive surgical procedures must obtain advice from their occupational health department and may need to be relocated to another work area.

Some health service employers have asked about HIV status as part of pre-employment screening. They have stated that they are acting in the best interests of applicants since this enables the provision of appropriate counselling and support to an infected nurse. However, others have argued that questions about HIV status are unethical because they are aimed at restricting employment opportunties for nurses infected with the virus. Proposers of this view state that the only legitimate concern of employers is the applicant's general physical health and ability to fulfil the job description.

HIV disease may cause extreme mental and physical debility and death. Many people affected by the virus are relatively young, articulate and have a strong desire to maintain control over their treatment and care. Their wish for control and a voice in the decision-making process may extend to the time when they are no longer capable of making informed choices. This has added to the interest in advance directives and living wills. Nurses need to contribute to the debate about the future roles these may play in health care, since helping people to have a dignified and peaceful death is essential to the nurses' caring and ethical role.

People affected by HIV and AIDS have also had an effect on medical research by successfully campaigning for increased access to drug trials and influencing study designs away from double-blind trials to give participants increased choice and information. Nurses have been involved in discussions around the ethics of unlinked anonymous HIV antibody testing and have a crucial role to play in ensuring that research protocols are not breached.

There are several other related ethical concerns that have been highlighted by the advent of HIV but for which there has not been space in this chapter. For instance, nurses caring for people with HIV and AIDS have been forced to address issues surrounding sexuality. Given that HIV is primarily sexually transmitted, what is the nurse's role in assessing and responding to patients' sexual knowledge, beliefs, values and behaviours? Should nurses be exploring these issues with all patients or only with those who are infected with HIV or who are considered to be at high risk of coming into contact with the virus? Issues such as these are not new as there have always been sexually transmitted diseases. However, research has shown that in the past nurses sought to avoid addressing such difficult issues (Webb 1985). The potentially catastrophic effects of AIDS, coupled with the increased emphasis on nurses' health promotion and illness prevention role, mean that such issues cannot be ignored. The identification of HIV and AIDS and sexual health as one of the government's five priorities in *The Health of the Nation* (1992) reinforces this point. Barker and Baldwin (DoH 1991) state:

> Raising questions about 'ethical issues' can, too often, be
> interpreted negatively as 'trouble-making'. In many
> situations, the 'trouble' already exists, in the form of
> inadequate or inappropriate services.

HIV and AIDS focus attention on a number of areas of health care which invoke ethical dilemmas and which nurses find 'difficult'. As such, by its very nature, AIDS is 'trouble-making'. On the positive side, AIDS has encouraged many nurses critically to explore their own attitudes, awareness and professional practice. This can be painful, as can all change. However, if this takes place in a safe and supportive environment, it can be viewed as an essential process through which nursing must pass in order to increase the standards of moral and practical care of all patients.

The construction of policies, procedures and standards of care is a necessary framework for approaching ethical problems. But the multifaceted nature of HIV demands a creative and flexible response from individual nurses to each situation which draws upon their relationship with the patients and places patients' interests at the heart of their practice.

References

Aggleton P J and Homans H (eds) (1988) *Social Aspects of AIDS.* Lewes: Falmer Press.

Akinsanya J and Rouse P (1991) *Who Will Care?* Faculty of Health and Social Work, Anglia Polytechnic.

Barker P and Baldwin S (eds) (1991) *Ethical Issues in Mental Health.* London: Chapman and Hall.

Bond S, Rhodes T, Philips P and Tierney A (1990) Knowledge and attitudes. *Nursing Times* **86**(45), pp 49–51.

Boyd K (1989) Ethical questions. In J Green and A McReaner (eds) *Counselling in HIV Infection and AIDS.* Oxford: Blackwell Scientific Publications.

Brown J M, Kitson A L and McKnight T J (1992) *Challenges in Caring: Explorations in Nursing Ethics.* London: Chapman and Hall.

Cranfield S and Dixon A (1990) *Drug Training, HIV and AIDS in the 1990s: A guide for training professionals.* London: Health Education Authority.

Department of Health (1991) *The Patient's Charter.* London: DoH.

Department of Health (1992) *The Health of the Nation.* London: HMSO.

Expert Advisory Group on AIDS (1991) *AIDS – HIV Infected Health Care Workers*. London: Department of Health.

Firn S (1991) HIV Testing and Informed Consent. *Nursing*, **4** (41), pp 35–6.

Fowler M D M and Chaney E A (1989) Ethical and legal issues. In J H Flaskerud (ed.) *AIDS/HIV Infection: A reference guide for nursing professionals*. Philadelphia: W B Saunders.

Gillespie F (1992) HIV/AIDS: The ethical and legal dilemmas. *British Journal of Nursing*, **1** (4), pp 197–200.

Hawkes N (1992) Helping AIDS along. *The Times*, 27 July, p 10.

Horton M (1989) Bugs, drugs and placebos: The opulence of truth, or how to make a treatment decision in an epidemic. In E Cater and S Watney (eds) *Taking Liberties: AIDS and cultural politics*. London: Serpents Tail.

Lyall J (1991) A slippery slope? *Nursing Times*, **87** (6), p 20.

Mansson S A (1990) Psycho-social aspects of HIV testing – the Swedish case. *AIDS Care*, **2** (1), pp 5–16.

Medical Defence Union (1989) *AIDS Medico-Legal Advice*. Cambridge: Medical Defence Union.

Miller R and Bor R (1989) *AIDS. A Guide to Clinical Counselling*. London: Science Press.

Morrison P and Burnard P (1991) *Caring and Communicating*. Basingstoke: Macmillan.

Pratt R (1991) Moral decision making in the age of AIDS. *Nursing*, **4** (34), pp 17–18.

Pyne R (1991) Legal and Ethical Issues of Paediatric HIV Infection. In R Claxton and T Harrison (eds) *Caring for Children with HIV and AIDS*. London: Edward Arnold.

Ross M and Seager V (1988) Determinants of reported burnout in health professionals associated with the care of AIDS patients. *AIDS*, **2**, pp 395–7.

Royal College of Surgeons of England (1990) *AIDS and HIV Infection*. London: Royal College of Surgeons.

Sadler C (1992) Positive reaction. *Nursing Times*, **88** (23), p 19.

Smith C (1992) Victims of a diseased society. *The Times, Saturday Review*, 8 August, pp 16–17.

Schlyter C (1992) *Advance Directives and AIDS: An empirical study of the interest in living will and proxy decision making in the context of HIV/AIDS care*. London: Centre of Medical Law and Ethics, King's College.

Thomas B (1990) Working out sexuality. *Nursing Times*, **86** (1), pp 41–3.

Tschudin V (1992) *Ethics in Nursing: The Caring Relationship*. Oxford: Butterworth-Heinemann, 2nd edition.

UKCC (1987) *Confidentiality: An Elaboration of Clause 9 of the Second Edition of the UKCC's Code of Professional Conduct*. London: UKCC.

UKCC (1992a) *Code of Professional Conduct*, 3rd edition. London: UKCC.

UKCC (1992b) *Acquired Immune Deficiency Syndrome and Human Immuno-deficiency Virus* (AIDS and HIV infection). Registrar's letter 24/1992. London: UKCC.

Wachter R M (1991) *The Fragile Coalition: scientists, activists, and AIDS*. New York: St Martins Press.

Webb C (1985) *Sexuality, Nursing and Health*. Chichester: John Wiley.

Annotated Reading List

Bury J, Morrison V and McLachlan S (1992) *Working with Women and AIDS: Medical Social and Counselling Issues*. London: Tavistock/Routledge.

Women now account for one-third of the ten million people with HIV infection worldwide. This book provides the latest medical information and a discussion of social issues, personal accounts and practical advice about ways of working with women affected by HIV and AIDS. Among the topics explored are contraception, pregnancy and HIV screening, prostitution and women who misuse drugs.

Claxton R and Harrison T (eds) (1991) *Caring for Children with HIV and AIDS*. London: Edward Arnold.

In addition to covering the broad range of subjects

relating to babies, children and young people with HIV infection and AIDS and their families, this book has an informative chapter on legal and ethical issues on paediatric HIV infection. Among the topics discussed are the status of minors, the relevance of international law and the sexually active HIV-positive minor.

Flaskerud J H (ed.) (1989) *AIDS/HIV Infection: a reference guide for nursing professionals.* Philadelphia: W B Saunders.

This concise edition was one of the first books available for nurses to include a chapter on ethics and legal concerns regarding HIV infection. Covered are the topics of obligation to treat, withholding and withdrawing treatment, mandatory testing and the rights of the nurse with HIV infection.

Tavanyar J (1992) *The Terrence Higgins Trust HIV/AIDS Book.* London: Thorsons.

This straightforward guide provides up-to-date information on HIV and AIDS and explores the issues they raise for all of us in our professional lives. The book discusses research and drug treatment, HIV and discrimination including employment issues, health assurance, housing and compulsory testing.

CHAPTER 4

Care of People with Long-term Illness

David Grant and Anne Manyande

This chapter concentrates on adult patients with long-term illness; children and the elderly are considered in other chapters in this book.

The fact that long-term illness means that there is no cure poses special problems for patients and carers. The psychological adjustment to this situation is as important as the physical adjustment. Several case histories show these aspects and the many ethical problems posed by them. The authors show these – from personal experience and wrestling with the problems – in the way that beneficence is a constant theme in this chapter.

Introduction

The concept of 'Long-term illness' encompasses a multitude of different conditions. Diabetes, chronic bronchitis and emphysema, epilepsy and heart disease are typical chronic conditions, which will be cared for by district and practice nurses. Although many of these patients will not have been affected by a long-term illness such as emphysema until they were in their forties or fifties, DiMatteo (1991) points out that young adults also experience long-term illness with surprising frequency. Sometimes the long-term illness may represent a condition such as epilepsy or Crohn's disease, which may not have been diagnosed until late adolescence or early adulthood. More

rarely, the long-term illness may present unexpected challenges. Patients with congenital conditions such as cystic fibrosis, or spina bifida and hydrocephalus may survive into adulthood because of advances in medical technology, and thus nurses may find themselves providing nursing care on a pioneering basis.

Irrespective of the age or the condition of the patient with a long-term illness, both the nurse and the patient are confronted by a single, unpalatable fact: chronic conditions by definition have no cure. This is one of the two central pillars to understanding the context within which nursing care for people with long-term illness is provided. The other is that most nursing care for the long-term ill will be delivered outside a hospital. Together, these two facts may provide an explanation as to why there is so little evidence that the medical specialist can do little more than the general practitioner or community nurse. They are also of prime importance in understanding the ethical dilemmas that confront those charged with providing nursing care to people with long-term illness.

The knowledge that there is no cure for virtually any long-term illness (for example, a heart transplant is a rare operation, and requires that the recipient be maintained for life on a regime of immuno-suppression) requires that the patient make a major psychological adjustment. This is neither simple nor necessarily predictable, even in instances where, outwardly at least, little has changed. For example, many individuals with epilepsy carry on in their work and domestic lives without even close colleagues, partners or children being aware of their medical condition. However, it would be a mistake to assume that a satisfactory psychological adjustment has taken place. Scambler and Hopkins (1988) reveal very clearly how an outer normality can conceal inner turmoil.

Stigmatisation

Scambler and Hopkins carried out detailed interviews with 94 adults with epilepsy living in the community. It is very clear from reading their report that people with epilepsy go to considerable lengths to pass as normal whenever feasible. Their concealment stems directly from a fear of stigmatisation. As one interviewee puts it, 'as soon as they know I'm epileptic they don't want to know me' (ibid.: p. 166). Consequently, most adults with epilepsy engage in concealment, often highly successfully. The extent to which many are successful can be judged from the fact that 1 in 200 of the population are on anticonvulsant medication for epilepsy in the United Kingdom at any one time, and yet most people are not aware that they may know of someone with this condition. However, the deliberate use of the subtitle 'A Dark Secret' in Scambler and Hopkins' review indicates the constant worry epileptics have of being, as it were, 'found out', and of the shame they would then experience.

As hospital specialists appear to be more interested in the management of epilepsy than in the social experience of being ill, providing effective nursing care for most epileptics requires that the legitimate fear of stigmatisation will have to be addressed by nurses to enable a satisfactory psychological adjustment to take place. The difficulties of

doing this should not be underestimated. The deep concern that epileptics have about coping with discrimination
because many people in the population hold a negative
stereotype of epileptics, requires a major attitudinal change
in the general population if this very real fear is to be
removed – a task beyond the scope of most district or
practice nurses. Maintaining confidentiality about a
patient's condition is paramount to the provision of effective nursing care. However, the extent to which confidentiality must be maintained may be called into question if
a patient with epilepsy engages in behaviours that pose a
genuine threat to public safety. Nurses who find themselves
in such a position are in an ethical dilemma.

   The issue of stigmatisation is an important one, for
nurses are not insensitive to the attitudes and stereotypes
that constitute part of the fabric of assumptions held by
the society within which they have grown up and work.
For example, caring for people with ill bodies, as is the
case with patients with rectal cancer, means overcoming
feelings of disgust about fecal matter and visual disfigure-
ment when dealing with a colostomy. Though training
will enable nurses to handle this condition in a matter-of-
fact way and training could help nurses to aid such patients
to come to terms with what these patients may see as a
very shameful stigma (see MacDonald 1988), the question
of the attribution of the cause of the condition is also of
importance. While it is unlikely that a patient with rectal
cancer will be perceived as being responsible for initiating
the condition, an alcoholic patient who becomes diabetic
or a person who develops AIDS may well be perceived in
more negative terms. In providing effective nursing care,
a nurse has to recognise that even though she or he may
disapprove of some behaviours that may have been the
cause of the development of a condition that requires
treatment – a disapproval that could well be echoed in
society at large – stigmatisation by the nurse is not con-

ducive to giving effective nursing care. The extent to which a nurse should deliberately mislead a patient in order to hide his or her disapproval of that patient is an ethical question.

Such disapproval can occur for a variety of reasons. It may arise because there are negative stereotypes held about various types of people (e.g. alcoholics). It could also arise because the patient engages in behaviours that may increase the severity of the condition, or because the patient is perceived as 'difficult'. Kelleher's (1988) work on non-compliance and coping strategies in diabetic patients is helpful in illustrating both issues. He points out that the high degree of non-compliance in diabetics may be explained by the juxtaposition of the strict demands of treatment and the fact that, at least in the short term, diabetes is (usually) neither a life-threatening condition nor one that produces severe pain. Treatment transgression is therefore fairly high (a good everyday example is that of dieting where treatment transgression is not only high but also usually incurs no social disapproval – unless the dieter has joined a group such as Weight Watchers). However, when dieting becomes part of a medical treatment regime, and transgression may worsen a condition, a nurse may well lose patience with a patient who persistently disregards dietary advice. However, as mentally capable adults enjoy a right to abuse their own bodies, if they exercise that legal right in a manner that conflicts with the requirement that nurses behave in a professional manner, this can and does give rise to an ethical dilemma. Even in cases where a diabetic patient does attempt to conform to a treatment regime, ethical dilemmas may still exist. Diabetics come to terms with their condition using a variety of strategies (Kelleher 1988). Whereas 'coping' and 'normalising' strategies are likely to result in a positive relationship between a nurse and the patient, the 'worriers and agonisers' are likely to test the nurse-patient relationship.

The question for nurses confronted with patients who test their patience to the limit is, at what point should another nurse attempt to establish a more effective relationship?

Ethical Dilemmas

The issues of non-compliance and quality of the nurse-patient relationship are likely to be less important in a hospital than for district or practice nurses. This is likely to be so for several reasons. First, it has often been observed that patients rapidly become 'institutionalised'. This in itself will help to ensure compliance and is in fact part of the phenomenon of institutionalisation. Second, there is a hierarchy of authority figures available. If the treatment advice of a ward nurse is not followed, more senior figures can be called in to reinforce that advice. These features of institutionalisation and ready access to authority figures are not available to a district nurse who sees a patient in his or her own home. In addition, as the district nurse may be the regular district nurse for a given community, most primary nursing care over time is likely to be delivered by the same person – unlike in a hospital where rotas and shift systems guarantee that a patient will be seen by a variety of nurses, to a point where the very diversity may threaten the delivery of good quality nursing.

Those who provide nursing care in the community are likely to experience certain ethical dilemmas far more frequently than if they were working in a hospital. As nurses working in the community are more likely to enjoy a degree of autonomy unknown within most hospitals, the resolution of ethical dilemmas is also likely to be more *ad hoc* unless there is an open discussion about key principles. The purpose of this chapter is to open that discussion and not to close it down with mechanistic solutions that do little to alleviate the various and complex challenges confronting those providing nursing care for the long-term ill.

Nurses will aim to maximise the patient's ability to live with his or her illness and to restore their sense of well-being despite the presence of illness. Because the social experience of living with a long-term illness can be acutely disturbing (as has already been illustrated in the case of epilepsy), the provision of education, of emotional support and of palliative intervention are of fundamental importance in seeking to enhance the quality of life for a patient, however that might be defined. As the notion of care is often seen in such terms as education (e.g. explaining and showing how to carry out a particular treatment), emotional support (e.g. via empathy) and palliative intervention (e.g. alleviating distress without being able to remove the cause), it is perhaps not surprising that Gillick (1984), as well as others, have focused attention on the importance of nursing over medical specialisms in the care of patients with long-term illness.

Even when the prime importance of nursing care is recognised – a recognition that, in terms of research, is long overdue – it is no easy matter to provide effective nursing care. Nursing care, whether it is in the provision of education, emotional support or in palliative intervention, is essentially a matter of achieving an effective psychological relationship with patients. Though there will be times when a nurse may respond with sympathy, pity or commiseration, these responses have been questioned and, in fact, called inappropriate, non-beneficial and even harmful (e.g. Knobbe 1989; Holden 1990). On the other hand, the response of empathy has been recommended as an appropriate, desirable and therapeutic response. Morse et al. (1992) go as far as to suggest that empathy is the central 'living component' in nurse–patient interactions. As the boundary between empathy and sympathy is not clear-cut, and there will be times when pity and commiseration will be effective ways of responding to a patient's needs, the nurse's decision how to respond in order to initiate and sustain a caring and supportive relationship will not be easily reached. These difficulties stem partially from the International Council of Nurses' Code for Nurses (1973). (We refer to this Code rather than the UKCC Code for it makes key ethical principles more explicit than the UKCC Code.)

Within that Code are four important ethical principles. The Code directs nurses to support self-determination by the patient – the principle of autonomy; to do good for the patient – the principle of beneficence; to avoid actions which will harm the patient – the principle of non-maleficence; and to respect the patient's rights and to seek fair treatment – the principle of justice. In order to be able to make and take effective and informed judgements, nurses must also be aware of current developments. What is acceptable and beneficial practice in one decade may well come to be seen as maleficent behaviour in another in the light of new knowledge. (A classic example is that of mother–infant bonding following birth.) Being up-to-date with current developments is the responsibility of the nurse, for it is clear from the UKCC Code of Professional Conduct (1992) that nurses should accept the responsibility and accountability of professional competence with all that that implies for remaining knowledgeable.

This is more easily said than done. Whereas changes in medical and clinical treatment may be communicated quickly to different sectors of the nursing profession, nursing care for the long-term ill is much more than this. Patients can respond in different ways to the same condition. What kind of nursing care would be most effective for each kind of response? It is a deeply regrettable fact that there is so little research on living with long-term illness. Even less research is available on how nurses can provide effective nursing care which recognises and responds to individual concepts to being ill. Those who are not nurses but of necessity assume responsibility for caring for those who are ill – a role typically taken on by a member of a family – could also be helped by such research. A nurse caring for the long-term ill will therefore experience considerable difficulties in providing effective nursing care. Not only is there a serious lack of empirical evidence to work from in developing nursing skills, but there is also a lack of channels for communicating swiftly any knowledge that will be derived from researchers who are likely to be of a psychological and sociological orientation. Their professional channels of communication are not necessarily those of the nursing profession. The current dearth of knowledge therefore forces a nurse to do what she or he believes to be right and to do so by relying to a considerable extent on gut feeling. The question of how to arrive at the right answer in the absence of adequate information implies a dependency on working within ethical principles.

The rather contentious observation was made above that some of the difficulties in working towards creating an effective and supportive relationship with a patient stemmed from the International Council of Nurses' Code for Nurses. This statement is no criticism of that Code. The ethical principles embodied within the Code are key principles and act as benchmarks by which to define key behaviours of the nursing profession. However, not all ethical principles can be adhered to on occasions, and there will be times when there are conflicts with other obligations. In the case-study scenarios that follow attempts will be made to illustrate and explore some of the ethical dilemmas that confront nurses who provide care for the long-term ill.

- John's social life had remained fairly constant for some time. On returning from work at about 6 o'clock he would watch

the early evening television, enjoy a leisurely cooked meal
and then, at about 8 o'clock, walk across the road to the
Working Men's Social Club and spend the evening with his
mates. Like many of them, his waistline had expanded
considerably since early adulthood. When teased about it
he would mutter rather defensively about his wife's belief
that he should have three square meals a day.

Because of his drinking habits John was used to getting
up in the night to urinate. However, following a period of
having his sleep disturbed rather more than usual, and the
need to urinate frequently persisting throughout the day,
he had reluctantly gone for a health check. This revealed
that he was diabetic.

John found coming to terms with his condition very
difficult. Having to control his eating and drinking was
very demanding and he attempted to deny his illness by
engaging in bouts of drinking. The diabetes nurse who
visited him regularly impressed on him the need for strict
restraint in his eating and drinking patterns, and the need
to maintain regular medication. While it was obvious to her
that his diabetic condition was worsening, his response, 'It's
my life and I'll do what I want with it', irked her considerably.
It irked his wife too. John was her life and she wanted to help
in any way she could.

Long-term nursing typically involves the care of patients
who live at home and often work. For many patients the
major challenge is accepting that that lifestyle has irrevo-
cably changed and that an attempt to revert to old habits
has medically negative consequences. Effective nursing
care therefore has to focus on helping the patient to accept
the need to modify his or her behaviour accordingly. This
implies an attitude change which may be difficult to bring
about. John's case study has been chosen to illustrate some
of the issues involved in nursing a non-compliant patient.

A key reason for focusing on Kelleher's (1988) work
early in this chapter is that his research highlights non-
compliance as being a notable and negative behaviour

typical of some diabetics. John's non-compliance is therefore not exceptional in one sense, though the degree of
self-abuse may be. Though his apparent self-denial of long-
term illness may be exceptional – and we stress the term
'may', for there is remarkably little research data available
– the self-abuse aspect of this scenario helps to make the
point that non-compliance can take different forms. In
many cases non-compliance may best be described as
benign neglect. In other cases non-compliance may appear
to be a deliberate attempt to reject advice and treatment.

It is essential to differentiate between benign neglect
and deliberate rejection because of the ethical implications.
The principle of autonomy provides for self-determination
by the patient. Therefore, non-compliance could be seen
as an act of self-determination by the patient, which should
be respected. However, there is a fundamental difference
between a patient who has deliberately chosen to reject
medical and nursing advice and a patient who has failed
to grasp the implications of not acting on such advice. For
a nurse to arrive at a conclusion that a patient has deliberately rejected advice requires a detailed consideration of
why that advice should have been rejected, and it is not
by accident that we used the phrase 'apparent self-denial'
in describing John's behaviour.

In seeking to understand why a patient is not complying
with a medical regime it is necessary to understand the
patient. It must be stressed here that this involves much
more than asking the patients why they aren't doing what
they have been asked to do. Such a line of questioning is
likely to fail in many instances because it is both too
narrow and presumes that the patients will be knowledgeable and articulate about their non-compliance. On the
other hand, such a line of questioning will succeed on
some occasions and therefore we do not wish to suggest
that asking this sort of question is inadvisable. Rather, it
is an opening question, not a closing question. To illustrate

why we stress the need to understand the patient in order to understand non-compliance we will now discuss two different types of non-compliance.

Benign Neglect

Before his diagnosis, John's lifestyle could hardly be said to be the epitome of healthy living. It would not be surprising if someone who has behaved with what can best be called benign neglect towards his or her personal health before a diagnosis carries on in the same way afterwards. In order to effect a change of behaviour it is necessary to appreciate that, in many cases, benign neglect might reflect a personal belief system that extends far beyond a response to a medical condition. A classic example of an early realisation of the importance of personal belief systems can be found in Douglas (1960). (If the phrase 'personal belief systems' had been current, he might well have used it.)

Douglas was the major name associated with the famous longitudinal study of all UK children born in the first week of March 1946. One aspect of that study focused on the development of premature children. In his 1960 analysis of the development of these children he drew a very strong association between poor educational achievement and parental attitudes, which are reflected in such maternal behaviours as not taking advantage of antenatal services, poor standards of maternal care and showing little interest in their child's school progress. The important point here is that one cannot take a behaviour in isolation. Rather, the totality of behaviours points towards a personal belief system that implicitly accepts a passive role that is at least partially a consequence of social and educational background. An appreciation of the fundamental importance of this background is crucial to understanding the context within which much of the long-term nursing will be provided, for the greater proportion of patients with long-term illness will be patients from the non-professional rather than the professional social categories.

For example, the standard mortality rate for deaths from diabetes is five times higher in women from social class V than for those from social class I (Davies 1991). This skewed distribution across social class is repeated for many different illnesses, from cervical cancer to bronchitis, and is found for both men and women. Davies makes the point that education is vital to bring about change, and there is little doubt that Douglas would concur with this. This is directly relevant to the provision of nursing care, for it stresses the need for nurses to act as educators. There are other implications as well. First, it would be reasonable to assume that the nurse should be proactive in providing this educational function; that is, information should be given automatically, rather than as an afterthought or only in response to questions. Second, and more complexly, it means accepting that the illness and non-compliance are not acts of wilful neglect. By accepting the first, the nurse will be working within the principle of beneficence. By accepting the second it could make the difference between responding with understanding and responding with frustration, thus avoiding transgressing the principle of non-maleficence. By accepting both it means that there is no clash with the principle of autonomy, for it implies that with appropriate nursing care, patients will change and behave in a manner that is compatible with maximising their ability to live with their illness.

The case is not so clear-cut in other instances of non-compliance. John's behaviour since his diagnosis could not be described as benign neglect. Rather, it appears to represent an active rejection of advice. Given this behaviour pattern, would a nurse be justified in accepting this as a clear example of a patient's right to determine whether he wishes to continue with treatment or not? In order to answer this question it means once again seeking to understand the reason for the behaviour. There is little evidence on how patients respond to being chronically ill, but what little there is suggests both 'compensatory behaviours of a self-assured and bustling kind' (Slijper 1984, p. 418) and a gender difference. If we generalise from the research by Slijper on children with diabetes mellitus and congenital adrenal hyperplasia (we freely acknowledge that such generalisations are questionable and point towards a research need) women are more likely to develop a more masculine style of behaviour – almost an act of denial – while men are more likely to become less masculine in their behaviours. Until there is better evidence, these generalisations have to be treated with considerable caution. Nevertheless, the point to make is that an active self-denial of illness should not necessarily be perceived as an act of wilfulness. It may represent a psychological response to being ill and as such will require responding to with understanding.

Beneficence

The principle of beneficence requires that a nurse seeks to do good for a patient. There can be no escape from this principle. Yet at the same time both the principle of autonomy and UK law stress the patient's independence. John is therefore legally justified in his comment, 'It's my life and I'll do what I want with it', and a nurse would have little option but to accept the truth of this statement. Nevertheless, the principle of beneficence requires that the patient cannot be abandoned, even if the patient has decided otherwise.

In seeking to provide effective nursing care for a patient who persistently ignores advice, the question has to be asked whether someone else may be better able to effect the change of behaviour that is being sought. Though it would be usual to refer this question as well as details about the patient's behaviour to someone in a senior position – and it could be seen as unprofessional conduct not to bring to the attention of a person senior to the nurse any patient behaviour that jeopardises that patient's well-being – the question of whether that other person could be someone closely associated with the patient is not usually discussed. However, a key distinguishing feature of nursing patients with long-term illness is that such care is delivered within the community, therefore the role of others associated with the patient is crucial if effective care is to be given. In fact, even working from the lowest estimates of that proportion of the population with long-term illness (10 per cent UK figures; Anderson and Bury 1988; cf. 50 per cent US figures; DiMatteo 1991), nursing care could not be delivered without non-medical support. Though these figures represent a pragmatic case for systematically involving others in the care of a patient, pragmatic cases do not necessarily represent solutions to ethical questions.

By going back to the key principles of beneficence and non-maleficence, the active involvement of others can be justified and, if this is the most effective means of enabling patients to function well in spite of their illness, not to involve people closely associated with the patients might be perceived as not acting in their best interests. For example, in John's case diet is all important. As his wife has played a significant role in preparing his meals for him, it is crucial that she is fully briefed on his new dietary regime and on what to do if he lapses into a coma. Without her active support, and here the educational function of the nurse is of vital importance, John has very little chance of being able to adjust to a new way of living. Though it could be argued that by educating John's wife the nurse is impinging on his autonomy, this argument

depends on whether one accepts that autonomy means freedom of self-determination without reference to anyone but the patient, or whether autonomy means freedom within constraints. These constraints will be explored in the next two scenarios.

- Carol's realisation that her life had changed for ever came when she was told by the consultant neurologist that she had epilepsy. Though the neurologist went to some trouble to explain that with appropriate medication she would be able to live a normal life, Carol could not accept this.

    Her persistent feeling that she was somehow 'mentally ill' troubled her immensely, and she went to great lengths to avoid telling anyone, including her fiancé. The practice nurse was the only person she felt she could confide in, and her worries about whether she should change jobs, or whether she could have 'normal' children, were broached with the practice nurse on more than one occasion. It was

during one of the sessions that Carol told the nurse that
she was getting married soon and had also been offered a
new job.

However, instead of being excited by the prospect of a
new life, Carol was deeply agitated. Her new job involved
a health check and, as getting married would coincide with
taking out a mortgage, she would also have to provide
health details to an insurance company. It was quite clear
to the nurse that Carol's fear of stigmatisation was such
that she had concealed her condition from both her fiancé
and her prospective new company. What now worried the
nurse was that Carol was indirectly inviting her to collude in
concealing her condition from those who might make
enquiries.

Carol's case differs from John's in several significant
aspects. First, she is complying with the medical regime
that has been prescribed. (Given her quite legitimate fear
of stigmatisation it is in her own interests to do so in order
to conceal her condition more effectively.) Second, she
has developed a high degree of trust and confidence in
her nurse. Finally, her wish for autonomy has public safety
implications. It is these latter two points that represent the
ethical dilemma for the nurse, and that allow us to expand
on the issue of autonomy.

Legal Rights

Under UK law patients have a right to refuse treatment if
they so wish. (This right holds true only for those whom
a court would deem mature and capable of reaching a
considered judgement. In addition, the right of a pregnant
woman to refuse treatment is currently the subject of legal
debate, but would appear to be legally actionable if she
refuses treatment that is expressly designed to aid the
unborn child.) Both John and Carol therefore have a legal
right to refuse treatment. There are, however, sets of cir-

cumstances recognised in law where the question of public safety is placed above the rights of the individual. Notifiable diseases constitute one such category. Pleas by patients that confidentiality be respected have a lower priority than the need to inform relevant statutory authorities and, in those rare instances where isolation (to prevent the spread of communicable diseases) is required, the rights of society are protected above the rights of the individual. While an individual may still refuse treatment, that individual can and will be held in isolation.

Carol's plea for confidentiality raises an important point. Epilepsy is not a notifiable condition. There is therefore no legal compulsion on the nurse to report this condition to a statutory body. Nevertheless, there are certain jobs that people with epilepsy may not occupy – usually by civil rather than criminal legislation – ranging from boxing to driving trains. Though the nurse in Carol's case can be expected to treat information provided in confidence, and in general terms would risk being charged with unprofessional behaviour if she were to divulge to others information passed on in confidence, the circumstances under which confidential information can be passed on will depend critically on the rights of others to know, and the wish of others to obtain information of a confidential nature. For example, the insurance company does not have a right of access to Carol's medical records, nor does her fiancé have a right to be informed by the nurse about his future wife's health status. The fact that she has deliberately concealed information from the company and her fiancé is a moral one, and a nurse who accepted without question such a concealment might reflect on the principle of nonmaleficence. It could be argued that the act of concealment could harm the patient if her fiancé has to deal completely unexpectedly with an epileptic fit and, lacking appropriate instruction, fails to handle the situation competently. Because concealment in this instance could harm the patient physically, there is a duty of care on the nurse at least to point out to Carol the possible consequences of concealment.

The question of psychological harm to a relationship, or a financial loss as a consequence of not providing full information, are more difficult issues. Though the fear of stigmatisation is a genuine one for many epileptics, a nurse cannot collude in actively supporting attempts at concealment where concealment may have negative consequences for the patient. Helping a patient to come to terms with an illness involves a supportive and educational role. In this case it would involve pointing out the consequences of concealment, but allowing Carol to reach her own *informed* decision, and then not breaking confidence if the decision is not one that the nurse agrees with.

The question of breaking a confidence becomes a critical one if Carol were to obtain a job that contains a prohibition on epileptics holding that job. Whereas Carol has a right to endanger her *own* life, she has no right to endanger the lives of others. The principle of autonomy is not absolute. The problem is that these are grey areas where a nurse has to exercise judgement as to what will constitute a defendable decision. A nurse providing care for a person with epilepsy should provide information about the kinds of activities which that person should not engage in, and circumstances which should be avoided. This should be seen as part of the nursing duty to provide information that will enable an epileptic to avoid harm. A nurse also has a duty to maintain confidentiality – not as an act of friendship but as a professional duty. However, a nurse is under no obligation because of a friendship to prevent disclosure of confidential information when there is a clear right for others to have access to that information, and it would be contingent on the nurse to explain this fact to the patient. The difficulty the nurse faces is one of preventing a nursing role becoming a policing role, for the rights of others are not always clear.

For example, if Carol had mentioned that she was applying for a position as a bus driver, the educative role of the nurse is clear. The inadvisability of applying for such a position must be explained and that if the employing company were to seek a medical statement, then her epileptic condition could not be hidden. It would also be important for the nurse to point out that the decision as to whether this information should or should not be divulged would not rest with the nurse but would be taken at a more senior level. However, her request for confidentiality would be noted and, with reference to other enquiries, such as the insurance company or her fiancé, confidentiality would be respected. The difference in principle between a right to know (i.e. the employing company for a prohibited position) and a wish to know (e.g. her fiancé) should be explained.

The concept of policing is a troublesome one. Suppose that in spite of the best advice of the nurse, Carol does obtain a position as a bus driver and, still living in the same community as the nurse, the nurse sees Carol driving. The nurse could take one of three courses of action. First, she could speak in confidence with Carol and remind her of the inadvisability of her having such a job. Second, she could raise it as a point of principle with more senior members of the nursing or medical team and seek advice. Third, she could report Carol's medical condition to the company so that the company could take action. Only the first of these potential courses of action breaks no code of confidentiality. If she takes the second course the nurse is reporting information that has, strictly speaking, no bearing on the medical condition. However, it resolves a moral dilemma in one sense in that it now becomes a shared dilemma. The issue here is one of the autonomy of the patient versus the safety of the community.

This issue is one that nurses will encounter on a number of occasions and experience difficulties in resolving. What should be remembered in such situations is that respect for the principle of autonomy does not imply an absolute obligation. Salladay and McDonnell (1992) point out that if we focus exclusively on individual rights, we may ignore equally important moral responsibilities to the family and community. A balance between individual autonomy and the rights of others has to be struck. While nurses should respect autonomy as a *prima facie* principle, they should also be aware that this principle may be overridden by another moral principle of greater weight or standing. A classic example was the unprecedented decision by a UK health team in 1992 to release the name of a man with AIDS. Their justification was that his sexual behaviour was such as to jeopardise the well-being of women within his community; it was alleged that in spite of knowing of his diagnosis he persisted in unsafe sexual practices and that he was promiscuous.

Though their decision meant breaking confidence it was felt that in this instance the moral obligation to others outweighed the obligations to respect the autonomy of the patient and the code of confidentiality. It should be noted that the team felt compelled to act in this way because of the lack of an appropriate legislative framework.

Carol's case has certain key similarities. The nurse is under no legal obligation to report Carol to her company, and if she does, Carol may claim that the nurse has transgressed both the code of confidentiality and failed to respect her right to act autonomously. In striking a balance between autonomy and the rights of others the seriousness of Carol's condition would be a key deciding factor which requires that a decision be reached by those best qualified to decide whether Carol's medical condition and her compliance with prescribed treatment are such as to minimise the risk of an epileptic fit while driving, or are almost certain to result in a major fit which could have serious consequences for others. It is not a question of one principle being a supreme principle. Rather, it is a question of balance. This will be explored further in the next two case studies.

- Mary had been diagnosed as having Crohn's disease at the age of 15. For a period of ten years her condition had been kept reasonably stable with drugs and, during that period, she married. When she was 25 the oral administration of cortisone and sulfasalazine were no longer effective and surgery became inevitable. She underwent a colectomy and an ileostomy, with the consequence that she then had to wear an external ileostomy bag. This was the first of many operations.

  Mary lost her self-esteem and self-confidence. Her husband felt physically sickened by the sight and smell of his wife's body and refused to share the same bed. Soon afterwards he left her and filed for divorce. Gradually, she became a social recluse and became more and more depressed. As her depression deepened, she began to talk openly about ending her life and it was with a sense of foreboding that the nurse continued to visit her. After the most recent operation the nurse had started visiting Mary every day. Because of her pain Mary had been prescribed analgesics but, because of concern that she might commit suicide, each analgesic prescription was quite limited. Nevertheless, the nurse had a strong suspicion that Mary was hoarding her analgesics in order to take her own life, even though Mary insisted that she was complying fully with the prescriptions. Because of this worry the nurse found herself spending more and more time with Mary, even though it was an experience she did not enjoy. At the same time, she felt that she could not undertake a search of Mary's flat to ascertain whether or not Mary was lying.

- Simon was a 60-year-old widower. He had recently been discharged from hospital following a heart transplant operation and was currently under the care of a community

nurse. His hypertension was being controlled by
vasopressors. Seven months after his heart transplant, he
was diagnosed as suffering from retinopathy and treated with
laser surgery. In spite of this his sight had deteriorated to
the point where he was registered blind.

The additional stress of coming to terms with his almost
complete loss of sight, plus his constant worry that he
might suffer another heart attack, meant that he was
unsuccessful at controlling his hypertension. In discussions
with the nurse about the possibility of another heart attack,
he had on several occasions expressed the wish that he
should not be resuscitated in the event of another heart
attack. The nurse was fully aware that Simon was 'of sound
mind' whenever he expressed his wishes about how he
wanted to be treated.

Three years after his heart transplant he suffered a
massive heart attack while the community nurse was
checking his blood pressure.

In both cases the nurse is confronted with a dilemma.
In the case of Mary, the nurse believes that Mary might
commit suicide and is hoarding part of her prescription to
enable her to do this. To engage in a surreptitious search
of Mary's flat might be seen as an invasion of privacy. Also,
in order to attempt to safeguard Mary, the nurse is spending more time than her medical – as opposed to her
psychological – condition warrants. In the case of Simon
the nurse is faced with the dilemma of whether to respect
Simon's wishes and therefore make no attempt to resuscitate him, or whether to go against his wishes and make
an attempt, not knowing whether it will be successful, and
if it were, what the consequences would be.

Though in each case the basic issue is one of the right
of the individual to decide the circumstances under which
that individual might die, the cases cannot be decided in
terms of a single overriding principle. The principle of
beneficence requires a nurse to do good for the patient;
this usually requires behaving in a way that saves and/or

prolongs life rather than end it ('beneficence' is generally used because specific circumstances exist when doing good will mean helping patients to die with dignity, such as in a hospice, or following a decision not to elect for active intervention). The question of whether seeking to prolong life (in the case of Mary and Simon) is doing good or not is not a simply answered question.

In the case of Simon, there is no doubt that he has clearly expressed his wish not to be resuscitated, and that he did so with an unimpaired mental capacity to reach a logical and reasoned decision. Notwithstanding this, not to intervene could nevertheless still result in Simon surviving the heart attack, but perhaps with brain damage. The principle of non-maleficence requires that a nurse act in a way that does not cause harm to the patient. Because the nurse in this instance is in a position of not knowing what the outcome of the heart attack will be, he or she should therefore work from the premise that no intervention may harm the patient and that the principle of non-maleficence overrides any other principles. If, having intervened, it is clear to the nurse that Simon's heart has stopped, further attempts to maintain life could then be withdrawn. As with previous scenarios, the question is one of striking a balance between ethical principles.

This is also the case in Mary's circumstances, but her scenario is rather more complex. While it could be argued that Simon's wish not to be resuscitated was clearly communicated and was one he arrived at as a mentally competent individual, the same is not true for Mary. While the nurse's suspicions of Mary's intent to commit suicide may be justified, they are, ultimately, just suspicions. Second, it could be argued that because Mary is so depressed she is not a mentally competent person. Therefore, even if she had communicated a wish to die, the principle of autonomy should not be invoked in her case.

The principle of non-maleficence is guiding the nurse's behaviour in this scenario.

Ideally, if Mary is likely to engage in a behaviour that is going to harm her, then a nurse should take all reasonable steps to protect her. The key to achieving a balance in this case is that of 'all reasonable steps'. In Mary's case there are two key elements. First, the nurse has to achieve a balance between the time she spends with Mary and the time she spends with other patients. The principle of justice requires nurses to seek fair treatment for their patients. By spending a great deal of time with Mary the nurse is likely to deny other patients their right to nursing support. While it is inappropriate for a nurse to allocate equal amounts of time to each patient, it would also be unreasonable to spend so long with one patient that the others then suffer. To do good to all patients on a nurse's list requires taking action to see that the needs of any one individual do not infringe on the legitimate needs of others. In this case it means decreasing the time spent with Mary even if this then increases the likelihood that Mary will attempt suicide. It is imperative therefore that the nurse's suspicions are communicated to others and the possibility of other support be investigated.

Second, 'all reasonable steps' rests on the distinction between when a person can legally be said to be capable of acting with autonomy, and when autonomy should be assumed by others. Though there is little doubt that many would accept that the present quality of life for Mary is poor, and some would even accept that if she wished to end her own life that wish should be respected, a nurse must distinguish between the legal right to autonomy and when autonomy for a person should be passed to another person or body, who can act in the best interests of that patient. Because this is a grey area in Mary's case, it is wise to seek further advice. Without such advice the nurse would be wise not to make a clandestine search for a suspected hoard of painkillers. The patient has a right to expect a nurse not to invade his or her privacy. While it would be professional for the nurse to enquire of the patient whether she is complying with the medical regime that has been prescribed, it would constitute an invasion of privacy if the nurse then undertook a search, having been informed by the patient that the regime has been followed. In the event of the patient informing the nurse that the regime has not been followed, it is essential that the person responsible for prescribing be informed. Without the consent of the patient a search still should not be undertaken, even if the intent is to prevent the person harming herself. The issues of autonomy, non–maleficence and of the right to privacy will also be explored in the next scenario.

- Sandra was born with spina bifida and hydrocephalus. Soon after her birth she had a ventricular shunt inserted to control her hydrocephalic condition. Her parents were told that, if she lived, she would be shunt-dependent for the rest of her life. Possibly because of the low level of her spinal lesion Sandra not only lived but was also able to attend a local school rather than attend a school for the physically handicapped.

  She enjoyed limited mobility and at primary school was able to walk with callipers. However, increasing obesity and a small degree of scoliosis had the effect of confining her to a wheelchair. Her IQ was about 90 (just below the population average). Urinary rather than fecal incontinence was an irritant but by learning a manual expression technique and, in her teens, learning how to self-catheterise, she had gained a degree of independence. This was important, for her mother died when she was in her early twenties, and a local housing association helped by providing a ground-floor flat.

  While her mother had been alive she had checked Sandra for bedsores each day. Following her death and Sandra's move to the flat, a district nurse had undertaken this task as well as questioning her about her health and continence management. One day, because of illness, an agency nurse was engaged to undertake the duties of the district nurse. On visiting Sandra he asked to check her for the presence of bed-sores. Sandra refused and when he started to enquire about how she was managing her continence, he was asked to leave. Soon afterwards the health centre received a phone call from Sandra who stated that she would only receive female nurses.

This scenario extends the discussion about privacy as well as introducing issues about agency versus full-time staff. In doing good for patients, respecting privacy is of importance. Given the psychological need of good nursing care, the establishment of trust between patient and nurse is therefore a prime consideration. In Mary's case searching her house for a suspected hoard of painkillers would have represented a breach of trust. In the case of Sandra, the privacy issue is that of to whom she is prepared to expose her body and answer intimate questions. In this case it is only to a woman and not to a man.

Professional Detachment

Because illness does not differentiate between intimate and non-intimate parts of the body, nurses learn how to handle intimate body parts with professional detachment. However, patients will not necessarily or easily discard their cultural or social heritage on becoming ill. There will therefore be times when nurses will be exposed to views and attitudes that will conflict with their need to behave with professional detachment. Just as there are some men who will perceive female nurses as sexual objects rather than caring professionals, and thus subject them to crude and lewd remarks, and may indeed invite nurses to engage in sexual behaviour when they are engaged in nursing intimate parts of their body, so there are some women who, for a variety of reasons, will find it objectionable to expose intimate parts of their body to male treatment or handling.

Within a hospital setting it would be relatively easy to provide either a same-sex nurse or request someone of higher authority to point out to a patient that certain behaviours of that patient are objectionable. (The term 'relatively' is used, because we cannot pretend that *all* nursing and medical staff are completely free of sexist or racist prejudices, or that *all* are ready to counteract such attitudes when they result in distress to nurses or others within a medical or nursing environment). Within a com-munity and visiting patients at home it is more difficult to arrange a substitute or bring pressure to bear on a patient whose behaviour is objectionable. Nurses are under a con-tractual as well as a professional duty to care for the patients they are assigned to (with the specific exemption of assist-ing at an abortion). They cannot therefore refuse to care for a patient, but a patient has a right to refuse such treatment. Sandra's case is different in that she is only refusing treatment from men, not from women. She still wants nursing support.

Though it may be difficult to provide alternative sup-port, practical difficulties should not cloud the issue of principle. By the health centre not seeking to provide alternative nursing cover – in this case a female nurse – Sandra may develop bed sores and thus suffer harm as a consequence. By their seeking to explore this issue with her and persuading her otherwise, Sandra may feel threatened and even suffer distress. For example, her anxiety about men may stem from a history of sexual abuse (there is documentary evidence that some people with spina bifida have been sexually abused) and she may not wish to discuss or explore this issue with anyone. In this case the principle of autonomy should be accepted without the nurse seeking to play an educative role about the consequences of not accepting a male nurse. It is not similar to the previous cases of John and Carol where the nurse is under an obligation to point out to non-compliant patients the consequences of their non-compliance. In this case explaining to Sandra the consequences of non-compliance may possible provoke mental distress and the principle of non-maleficence becomes paramount.

Non-Maleficence

The issue of agency nurses is separate from that of the refusal of a patient to be treated by a specific nurse. Nevertheless the principle of non-maleficence needs exploring for two reasons: continuity of care, and stereotyping. The concept of continuity of care is important both to the training of nurses and to the deliverance of good nursing. In nursing the long-term ill it will be inevitable that because of holidays and/or sickness, patients within a practice or area will not always be seen by the same nurse. Nevertheless continuity of care will usually be the predominant practice. However, there will be some circumstances when agency nurses will be called in. If this occurs on other than a short-term basis, then continuity of care will be broken and the question of whether the lack of continuity is harmful to the patient should be addressed. However, it could be addressed in another way.

Agency care usually means that agency nurses have very little time to get to know their patients. They are therefore likely to use stereotypes of patients to guide their behaviours. It is all too easy to think in terms of a typical diabetic, bronchitic or epileptic. Time constraints prevent agency nurses from developing an individualistic knowledge of patients. It is our judgement that for this reason, agency nurses are much more likely to approach patients stereotypically rather than individualistically. Use of agency nurses other than as emergency cover should therefore be questioned in terms of the principle of non-maleficence.

Values

Early on in this chapter, the different coping responses adopted by diabetics were discussed, as well as the need to look behind the behaviour in order to understand. By acting in this manner a nurse will demonstrate a respect for the individual. What has not yet been explored is the question; at what point does a nurse who seeks to deliver individualised nursing care that reflects respect for the values of the patient start to deliver poor nursing care? This is a question of some importance for nurses who deliver nursing care within the community. The term community is rather misleading because it suggests that there is just one community, whereas the reality is that different communities exist. Within a relatively small area a nurse can encounter patients from different social groups and ethnic backgrounds. This diversity can result in a nurse encountering very different values attached to behaviours. The last scenario explores this issue.

- Steve's high blood pressure and chronic bronchitis had progressively worsened over the past ten years and had reached a point where even going upstairs had become a major challenge. He had smoked regularly from his teens onwards, though he claimed that he had given up several years ago. The district nurse had her doubts about this. Steve was self-employed and ran a shop. Though he was unable to play an active part in serving and putting the stock out, he still took an active interest in financial matters. He would often get excited or angry by relatively trivial matters. Advice to him to relax and to take things easy appeared to have no effect.

> One day, when visiting Steve, the nurse walked in just as he commenced a prolonged coughing attack. Lying nearby on the floor was a half-smoked cannabis joint. After the nurse had helped him breathe more easily, he explained that he was only following advice to relax. The occasional joint, he claimed, did his blood pressure a world of good.

There are some communities which attach positive rather than negative values to smoking cannabis. The nurse may not share these values, but he or she may encounter such beliefs. In this case Steve is also engaged in an illegal activity. Because of the injunction to confidentiality in the UKCC Code of Professional Conduct, 1992 (clause 10), the nurse would be obliged, in a circumstance such as this, to keep such information confidential (though we have already discussed instances where a moral principle can override this code in exceptional circumstances). The question for a nurse is one of whether a given behaviour will impact positively or negatively on the patient's illness. By going back to the two principles of autonomy and beneficence, the question can be reformulated. By seeking to do good to the patient, do you find that the principle of autonomy has to be overridden at times?

Steve is exercising his right to autonomy by engaging in a behaviour which he claims is beneficial. It is also a behaviour which, although illegal, is acceptable in some communities or age cohorts. In seeking to respect the views of an individual a nurse necessarily has therefore to distinguish between her or his own values and good nursing practice. In this instance the nurse has to take care not to criticise Steve's behaviour as this would be perceived by him as a negative comment on his cultural values. Rather, comments have to be delivered in a manner that makes it clear that the nurse believes that his behaviour is bad for his medical condition. This distinction is necessary if the patient is to respond positively to the educational role that the nurse is engaged in. There is also an implication here for the nurse. Through keeping abreast of the literature the nurse could offer practical advice on how to reduce stress without resorting to illegal (or legal, in the case of alcohol) substances.

The delivery of effective nursing care to patients with long-term illness is a major challenge, not least because of the diversity of settings within which a nurse will care for patients, and the high degree of independence a nurse will be expected to demonstrate. The challenges will not be posed by a lack of medical knowledge. Rather, they will be posed by the psychological and cultural needs and values of individuals, and the social milieu that is an integral part of their family and peer network. In reaching for effective responses, as we have sought to show here, efficacy will partially be determined by working in an informed and consistent manner within a framework of ethical principles.

References

Anderson R and Bury M (eds) (1988) *Living with Chronic Illness: The experience of patients and their families.* London: Unwin Hyman.

Davies B M (1991) *Community Health and Social Services,* 5th edition. Sevenoaks: Edward Arnold.

DiMatteo M R (1991) *The Psychology of Health, Illness, and Medical Care: An individual perspective.* California: Brooks/Cole.

Douglas J W B (1960) 'Premature' children at primary schools. *British Medical Journal,* 2 April, 1008–13.

Gillick M R (1984) The care of the chronically ill: a medical prerogative? *New England Journal of Medicine,* Vol. 310, III, 190–3.

Holden R J (1990) Empathy: the art of emotional knowing in holistic nursing care. *Holistic Nurse Practice,* 5, 70–9.

ICN (1973) *Code for Nurses*. Geneva: International Council of Nurses.

Kelleher D (1988) Coming to terms with diabetes: coping strategies and non-compliance. In R Anderson and M Bury (eds) *Living with Chronic Illness: The experience of patients and their families*. London: Unwin Hyman.

Knobbe T M (1989) Pity doesn't help patients. *Research Nurse*. **52** (7), 21–2.

MacDonald L (1988) The experience of stigma: living with rectal cancer. In R Anderson and M Bury (eds) *Living with Chronic Illness: the experience of patients and their families*. London: Unwin Hyman.

Morse J M, Bottorff J, Anderson G, O'Brien B and Solberg S (1992) Beyond empathy: expanding expressions of caring. *Journal of Advanced Nursing*, **17**, 809–21.

Salladay S A and McDonnell M N (1992) Facing ethical conflicts. *Nursing*, February, 44–7.

Scambler G and Hopkins A (1988) Accommodating epilepsy in families. In R Anderson and M Bury (eds) *Living with Chronic Illness: the experience of patients and their families*. London: Unwin Hyman.

Slijper F M E (1984) Androgens and gender role behaviour in girls with congenital adrenal hyperplasia (CAH). In G J De Vries et al. (eds) *Progress in Brain Research*, Vol. 61. Amsterdam: Elsevier.

UKCC (1992) *Code of Professional Conduct*, 3rd edition. London: United Kingdom Central Council for Nursing, Midwifery and Health Visiting.

Index